TRANSLATIONS OF CHRISTIAN LITERATURE
SERIES II
LATIN TEXTS

GENERAL EDITORS: W J. SPARROW-SIMPSON, D.D,
W. K LOWTHER CLARKE, B.D.

TERTULLIAN

AGAINST PRAXEAS

TRANSLATIONS OF CHRISTIAN
LITERATURE . SERIES II
LATIN TEXTS

TERTULIAN AGAINST PRAXEAS

BY

ALEXANDER SOUTER, D. LITT.

WIPF & STOCK · Eugene, Oregon

Wipf and Stock Publishers
199 W 8th Ave, Suite 3
Eugene, OR 97401

Tertullian Against Praxeas
By Souter, Alexander
Softcover ISBN-13: 978-1-6667-3388-4
Hardcover ISBN-13: 978-1-6667-2920-7
eBook ISBN-13: 978-1-6667-2921-4
Publication date 8/12/2021
Previously published by SPCK, 1919

This edition is a scanned facsimile of
the original edition published in 1919.

IN
LOVING MEMORY
OF
MY DAUGHTER
BETH
SUDDENLY
CALLED TO HIGHER SERVICE
IN HER SIXTEENTH YEAR
DECEMBER 15, 1918

PREFACE

BY common consent the *Against Praxeas* of Tertullian is one of its author's most important works. Like many other writings which have sprung out of controversy, it possesses a positive and historic significance also, as the earliest surviving formal statement of the doctrine of the Trinity. It is true that the argument, at least so far as it is based on passages from the Greek version of the Old Testament, or on a Latin translation of that Greek, is not so convincing to the modern student of Scripture as it must have been in Tertullian's own day. Yet the knowledge of the Bible shown is amazing, and such as to shame most modern readers. At the same time the sheer brain power which the work exhibits would render it notable in any age.

The difficulty of interpreting Tertullian is an old story. There is no Latin writer for whose study an exhaustive concordance or special lexicon is so necessary, and yet there are few for whose Latinity so little of a comprehensive nature has been done. With the exception of the complete vocabulary of the works edited in the two volumes of the

Vienna edition, preserved in Munich for the sake of the great *Thesaurus Linguae Latinae,* and Henen's published index to the *Apologeticus*, no complete record of the vocabulary of a single work of Tertullian is known to me. The translator has therefore to depend on the incomplete indexes of words in the various editions and the useful, if necessarily partial, treatment of the vocabulary in Hoppe's *Syntax und Stil des Tertullian*. It is fortunate, however, for the translator of the *Adversus Praxean* that his difficulty arises more from individual terms of theological import like *substantia*, than from the build of clauses or sentences.

Here, too, as in the case of Tertullian's works generally, we are faced with a scanty manuscript tradition of somewhat questionable value. Gratitude is due to Dr. Emil Kroymann for the fresh record of manuscript variants in his two editions (Vienna, 1906; Tubingen, 1907). I have not been able to adhere, however, either to his or to any other single text. In particular I would deprecate the theory underlying Kroymann's frequent additions to, and excisions from, the text of the manuscripts. Words do get lost and added in the course of transmission, but if I may venture to say so, hardly in the way Kroymann postulates. I have consulted in addition to Kroymann, the complete editions of De la Barre (Paris, 1580), Rigault (Paris, 1634), and Oehler (Leipzig, 1854). I have also profited by the notes on the text of chapters 1–17, contributed by Dr C. H. Turner to the

Journal of Theological Studies, vol. xiv. (1912–1913) pp. 556–564. The monograph of d'Alès, *La Théologie de Tertullien* (Paris, 1905), has proved most valuable to one who is no theologian I have not seen any previous English translation, but I was glad to accept the kind offer of my assistant, Mr. James H. Baxter, M.A., of Glasgow University, to revise my translation, before I had revised it myself. I have been at pains to record the Biblical quotations and references with greater fulness than the editors. My book is not intended for the expert in Tertullian; he may, however, find something in the notes to interest him. The general reader is expected to use the translation along with the original, but I hope it will be intelligible even to readers for whom the original is a closed book.

A. SOUTER.

Aberdeen,
    February 8, 1919

INTRODUCTION

§ 1.—On Tertullian's Life and Works

OF Tertullian, as of many another who has rendered pre-eminent service to humanity, almost nothing is known. His full name was Quintus Septimius Florens Tertullianus, and he was a native of the Roman province of Africa, which corresponded roughly in area to the modern Tunis. He was of pagan parentage, and underwent a complete training as a lawyer. He appears to have visited Italy, but he spent the greatest part of his life in the city of Carthage, which had been refounded by Julius Caesar about a hundred years after the younger Scipio had laid it waste. The city had become once again a great centre, and Christianity must have reached it at an early period, probably direct from Italy. In Africa the new religion found a favourable soil, a fact not altogether undue to the Semitic origin of the old Punic stock, which found something akin to itself in the daughter of Judaism. The number of churches in Africa in Tertullian's time probably greatly exceeded the total of Italy itself. And this Christianity seems to have been more Latin than Greek. The most highly educated of the provincials in Africa were acquainted with Greek, but the proportion of such persons was far less than would have been found in Italy.

We have no evidence as to the date of Tertullian's birth, but if we place it about A D. 160, we shall probably not be far wrong. The date of his conversion is equally unknown, but it may be assigned to the period of mature manhood. He was a man of ardent temperament, unbounded energy and great creative faculty. In such a man conversion was sure to be followed at the earliest possible interval by active work on behalf of the Faith, and for him the pen was the obvious instrument. All his knowledge of law, literature and philosophy was at once enlisted on the side of the persecuted religion. Like a later convert from paganism, St. Ambrose, he must have taken up the study of the Scriptures as eagerly as he had followed his earlier pursuits. We have no satisfactory evidence that he held any office in the Church. It is safest to regard him as an early forerunner of a succession of Christian laymen, men like Pelagius, Marius Mercator, Junilius and Cassiodorus, who have had their share in building up the body of Christian doctrine

The strongly ascetic vein in Tertullian led him later to adopt the doctrines of the Montanists. This sect took its name from Montanus of Pepuza in Phrygia, and among its tenets was the assertion of prophetic gifts in opposition to the regularly constituted ministry, millenarism, and abstinence from every sort of union between the sexes. The influence of Montanism spread gradually in the West, and reached Africa almost certainly from Italy, but it is improbable that it had become associated with a declared sect in Africa in Tertullian's time. It represented rather a tendency within the bosom of the Church. But that tendency gained more and more power with Tertullian himself, and in his later works he accepts the doctrine of the new prophecy, and inaugurates the arbitrary rule of individual spiritual gifts, thus undermining the authority of the Old and New Testaments as well as that of the Church. He contradicts Scripture in urging the Christian to face persecution, in depreciating marriage, in making regulations for fasting, and other minor matters.

But these and other exaggerations, though they have deprived Tertullian of canonisation, in no way affect his importance as the earliest of the Latin Fathers. His great learning, his obvious sincerity and his burning eloquence are to be set over against such excesses, as well as against the occasional coarseness which will break out in the writings of a Tertullian, a Jerome and an Augustine, who have in their unregenerate days become too familiar with uncleanness. In originality he is inferior to none of these. In doctrine and in language alike he is a pioneer of Western Christianity. To him we owe the first formulation of the doctrine of the Trinity, to him we owe a great part of the Christian Latin vocabulary. He is the earliest Latin writer to quote Scripture with any freedom, and he is the first of that roll of noble names, Tertullian, Cyprian, Hilary, Ambrose, Jerome, Augustine, which no Christian literature in any language can match.

Yet here, also, we have our treasure in earthen vessels. Tertullian is the most difficult of all Latin prose writers, outdoing the fully developed Tacitean style in that brevity which inevitably becomes obscurity. His vocabulary is curiously compounded of technical legal language, Grecisms and colloquialisms, and in the absence of a special lexicon or a concordance to his works it is a task of extreme difficulty at times to ascertain precisely what shade of meaning to assign to a word. The importance of Tertullian is becoming so widely recognised now that the task of compiling such a lexicon may be commended to a patient scholar as one of the most urgent requirements of Latin scholarship. But we shall never know his vocabulary and idiom in the way that it is possible to know that of Jerome, Augustine or Gregory. The comparative neglect of his works in the Middle Ages has resulted in the survival of a pathetically scanty list of good manuscripts. Much of his text will, in consequence, never be restored with absolute certainty.

The list of his surviving works, with the dates now generally [1] assigned to them, is as follows:—

---

[1] I follow d'Alès, pp xiii ff., slightly different from Harnack, *Gesch. altchr Litt.*, II 2. (Leipzig, 1904), pp 295 f.

Ad Martyras	Feb. or March 197.
Ad Nationes	after Feb. 197.
Apologeticus	autumn 197.
De Testimonio Animae	between 197 and 200.
De Spectaculis	about 200.
De Praescriptione Haereticorum	about 200.
De Oratione	
De Baptismo	
De Patientia	
De Paenitentia	
De Cultu Feminarum	between 200 and 206.
Ad Uxorem	
Adversus Hermogenen	
Adversus Iudaeos	
De Virginibus Velandis	about 206.
Adversus Marcionem, Libri I.–IIII.	207–8.
De Pallio	209.
Adversus Valentinianos	
De Anima	
De Carne Christi	
De Resurrectione Carnis	between 208 and 211.
Adversus Marcionem, Liber V	
De Exhortatione Castitatis	
De Corona	211.
Scorpiace	211 or 212.
De Idololatria	211 or 212.
Ad Scapulam	end of 212.

INTRODUCTION

The following are definitely Montanist:—

De Fuga in Persecutione	213.
Adversus Praxean	⎫
De Monogamia	⎬ after 213.
De Ieiunio	⎭
De Pudicitia	between 217 and 222.

Besides these, several works by him have been lost. It is also to be noted that he issued the *Apologeticus* (probably) and the *De Spectaculis* (certainly) in Greek, as well as a Greek work on Baptism.

Of annotated editions of Tertullian's complete works, the best is that by Franciscus Oehler (Lipsiae, 3 Vols, 1853, 1854). The best text of the following works is to be found in the Vienna *Corpus Scriptorum Ecclesiasticorum Latinorum*, Vols. XX. and XLVII. (Vindobonae et Lipsiae), 1890, 1906) : *De Spectaculis, De Idololatria, Ad Nationes, De Testimonio Animae, Scorpiace, De Oratione, De Baptismo, De Pudicitia, De Ieiunio, De Anima, De Patientia, De Carnis Resurrectione, Adversus Hermogenen, Adversus Valentinianos, Adversus Omnes Haereses,*[1] *Adversus Praxean Adversus Marcionem* The best work on the language of Tertullian is H Hoppe, *Syntax und Stil des Tertullian* (Leipzig, 1903) ; on his theology, A. d'Alès, *La Théologie de Tertullien* (Paris, 1905); on his New Testament citations, H. Ronsch, *Das Neue Testament Tertullian's* (Leipzig, 1871).

[1] This book is perhaps the work of Victorinus of Pettau († 303).

INTRODUCTION

§ 2.—ADVERSUS PRAXEAN [1]

Of the life of Praxeas almost nothing is known. We may safely argue that he was a Greek, for the name is Greek and not Latin. He lived and taught at Rome early in the third century, sharing the views of a contemporary, Noetus of Smyrna. He gained some reputation in the metropolis for his exposure of the Montanist prophets, and would thus be far from acceptable to an adherent of their views like Tertullian. But Praxeas' services in this connexion were counterbalanced by heresy in another. He insisted on divine unity to such a degree that he destroyed the Trinity. Crudely expressed, his position was that the Father alone was God, and that all the experiences undergone by Jesus in His earthly life were undergone by the Father. The other two Persons in the Trinity were reduced to mere modality. Praxeas later recanted, but his heresy was to spring up later with Sabellius, from whose name it comes to be called Sabellianism.[2]

Tertullian does not find it difficult to make a very vigorous defence of the doctrine of the Trinity, a defence which loses none of its importance and value from the fact that the author was

---

[1] In this section I am greatly indebted to d'Alès, pp 67–81. Compare also Bp Kaye, *The Ecclesiastical History of the Second and Third Centuries* (cheap edition), pp 260–280; Blunt, *On the Right Use of the Early Fathers* (London, 1857), pp 485–517

[2] It is also, of course, known as Patripassianism, which may be paraphrased "the doctrine that the Father suffered (on the Cross)."

a Montanist at the time he wrote it. He points out Praxeas' contention that it was the Father Himself who was incarnated in the Virgin, that it was He who was born and suffered, that the Father is Jesus Christ. The Christian tradition, however, without surrendering the unity of the Godhead, maintains the "economy" (*oeconomia, dispensatio*) of the Trinity. God is one, but His activities are exercised by Father, Son and Spirit. There is one Son of God, His Word, incarnated by Him, who in His turn sent the Holy Spirit or Paraclete who comes from the Father, to sanctify in the faith those who believe in the Father and the Son and the Holy Spirit. This is the faith of the Gospel, the creed of the Church. Tertullian does not, however, rest content with this statement. He proceeds to elaborate a proof of it, and he begins by pointing out that divine unity is not in question, because the Church admits one divine substance in three persons, Father, Son, and Holy Spirit. They are one substance; they differ only in degree, form, aspect. The rest of the treatise (chap. 3 to the end) is only a development of this thesis.

Ordinary Christians hold fast to the idea of "monarchy," from fear of polytheism. Tertullian analyses the idea of monarchy and points out how in the case of an earthly monarchy the power of the sole ruler is not impaired by devolution of certain powers to his subordinates. It is his power all through, and they are the essential instruments of it. So it is with the hierarchy of heaven. The Son must restore His kingdom to the Father (1 Cor. xv. 24, 25, 28). A full study of all the Scripture references to the Son is, however, necessary. God existed alone at the beginning of the world, but He already carried His thought (*ratio*, *sensus*) within Himself; this is what the Greeks mean by *Logos*, which the Latins have represented by *Sermo*. In His thought was His Word, which by mental effort He made distinct from Himself.

This same divine thought is called Wisdom (*Sophia*) in the Book of Proverbs (viii. 22 ff.),[1] where we find the second person carrying out the plan of God's works. This thought is developed through a synthesis of a number of passages of Scripture. The Word is substance, He is person, He is Son of the Father, and has the highest position after Him. A possible confusion with Valentinus the Gnostic's doctrine is here elucidated, by showing clearly the difference between his position and that of the true thinker, in particular the real union between the Father and Son, which is copiously illustrated, especially from St. John's Gospel. The relation of Father to Son is compared to that of the tree and its branch, the source and the river, the sun and a ray of the sun. Keeping the analogy, he compares the Holy Spirit to the fruit on the branch. We must hold fast to the indissoluble union of Father, Son and Holy

[1] *Prax.* 6.

Spirit. Yet the Father and the Son are different, in that the Father is greater than the Son. The Holy Spirit is also other than the Son, for the Son promised to send Him. A father implies a son, and a son a father; to fail to recognise this is to destroy the Father as well as the Son God can do everything, but He did not will everything, and with Him to will is to do. Scripture proves separate identity of the three Persons by introducing one speaking to another,[1] as well as by the occasional use of the plural number [2]

Tertullian then meets the accusation that these passages prove the existence of two gods. Scripture has often given the name God to the three Persons taken separately, but Christians are careful never to speak of "gods" in the plural, lest they should be charged with polytheism. The distinction between the Divine Persons is also proved by the divine appearances in the Old Testament. The Son as God is as invisible as the Father, the Son is visible only as Man. The theophanies of the Old Testament imply a created mediator, namely the Son. The reference to God appearing to Moses "face to face" (Numb. xix 6–8) is taken, with Irenaeus,[3] as referring to the Transfiguration by anticipation, and in Old Testament times the Son appeared only "in an image or enigma"

In the New Testament we find it stated more

---

[1] *Prax.* 11. [2] *Prax.* 12.
[3] *Adv Haer.* V. 20, § 9.

INTRODUCTION xxi

than once that no one has seen the Father, yet there we find equally definite statements that the Son has been seen and even touched. And it was not only after the incarnation that this took place. the Divine appearances of the Old Testament are appearances of the Son. There is no difficulty in supposing that He acted in the Father's name, for the Father shares everything with Him.

The Monarchians appeal, however, to some passages where monotheism is strongly insisted on, for example, Deut. xxxii. 39, John x. 30, xiv. 9–11. But they are really founding their doctrine on a few obscure passages to the exclusion of many others that are perfectly clear. To these few passages Tertullian opposes in detail a large number from the Gospels, which represent two distinct Persons. He points out how a passage like John x. 30, instead of supporting their view, actually tells against it. There is moral and dynamic union between the three Persons, but unity of substance is also clearly affirmed with reference to the Paraclete (John xvi. 7, 14), who receives His substance from the Son, as the Son receives His from the Father. The story of the childhood of Jesus equally proves the distinction between the Father and the Son. According to Tertullian, the expressions *spiritus dei*, *virtus altissimi* (Luke i. 35), would indicate the Son. *Spiritus dei* and *Sermo dei* would be in effect two names, the one referring to substance, the other to activity, to indicate the one Person of the Word Son of God.

But the Monarchians, even when compelled by Scripture to distinguish the Son from the Father, destroy the effect of their admission by finding in the one person of Jesus Christ both the Son (that is, the human being Jesus) and the Father (that is, the spiritual being God who is also the Christ). But the Acts of the Apostles establishes that Jesus is surnamed the Christ because He is the anointed of the Father, which is another proof that the Father is not the Christ (Acts iv. 27). St. Peter, St. John, and St. Paul are also cited in evidence that the Father and Son are to be distinguished. The most decisive texts are those that mention the death of Christ, Son of God [1] (1 Cor. xv. 3). Christ being composed of two substances, the one divine and immortal, the other human, could die according to the flesh alone. And here appears the error of those who make the Father die on the cross. The Father being God only, could not die, nor could He bear the curse attached to crucifixion. This fact condemns the Patripassians and even the Patricompassians. For, being unable to prove that the Father suffered, some try to make out that He was a fellow-sufferer. But this view after all implies suffering on the Father's part, and the principle must be laid down that the Father is impassible. And the Son also is impassible as far as His divinity is concerned. He suffered as man, but the man

[1] *Prax* 29.

in Him was separated from the Father, while the God in Him was still united with the Father. To trouble the water of a stream is not necessarily to trouble the source: yet it is the water from the source that flows in the bed of the stream, and the stream is not separated from the source. Even if the divinity in the Son had suffered, this suffering could not have flowed back to the Father. But there is no need to dwell on this supposition, for the divine spirit as such did not suffer Although the Son suffered in His flesh, the Father was in Him, but did not suffer. Similarly, in proportion, we can suffer for God, thanks to the Divine Spirit which is in us yet the Divine Spirit does not suffer. Tertullian's last argument is perhaps his most powerful—a reference to the words of Christ dying on the cross. "My God, why hast thou forsaken me?" It is not the God we are listening to here, but the man who cries to an impassible and inflexible God. These words are the effect of the inexorable sentence which delivers His human nature to death. He delivers up His human soul into His Father's hands, and expires. Raised by God's power, He ascended to heaven, where Stephen saw him on the Father's right hand. One day He will come on the clouds. Meantime, He has sent the Holy Spirit, the third Person of the Trinity, for the full revelation of the Christian mystery. To refuse to believe in the Trinity, is to become a Jew. It is this doctrine alone that separates us from the Jews. it is the work of the Gospel, the kernel of the New Testament. God who revealed Himself but obscurely in the Old Testament, preserved for these later days this great light on His real being. He who will have life, must believe on the Son of God.

TERTULLIAN AGAINST PRAXEAS

1. MANIFOLD are the ways in which the devil has shown his enmity to the truth He has at length striven to shatter it by defending it. He claims that there is but one God, the all-powerful Creator of the universe, in order to make a heresy even out of that one. He says that the Father Himself descended into the virgin, that He likewise was born of her, and Himself suffered ; even that He Himself is Jesus Christ. The serpent forgot himself, for when trying Jesus Christ after He had been baptised by John, he approached Him as Son of God, knowing full well that God had a Son, even from the very Scriptures out of which he was then building up the temptation.[1] " If thou art the Son of God, speak that these stones become loaves " ; again . " If thou art the Son of God, cast thyself down hence , for it is written, that He "— that is, the Father—" hath given His messengers charge over thee, to uphold thee by their hands lest anywhere thou shouldst strike thy foot against a stone." Or shall he upbraid the Gospels with falsehood, and say . " It is Matthew's and Luke's

Matt. iv. 3

Matt. iv 6
cf. Luke iv. 9–11

---

[1] For the missing present participle of *sum* to be supplied with *certus*, cf. Hoppe, pp 144 f

concern, not mine? It was God Himself that I approached, the All-powerful Himself whom I assayed hand to hand, it was for that reason that I approached, it was also for that reason that I attacked. But if He had been merely the Son of God, I should never have deigned to tempt Him." In truth, however, it is rather "he himself" who "has been a liar" "from the beginning," he and any man he has privily sent of his own accord, such as Praxeas. For it was Praxeas who first, from Asia,[1] imported this kind of perversity to Roman soil, a restless being in other [2] respects, and puffed up besides with boasting about his martyrdom, which consisted merely in an ordinary brief, if irksome,[3] period in prison; whereas, even if he had "surrendered his body to be burnt up," it would have "profited him nothing," as he had not "the love" of God, whose "gifts" he even violated. For, when the then bishop of Rome [4] was now recognising the prophecies of Montanus, Prisca and Maximilla, and as the result of that recognition

cf. John viii. 44

cf 1 Cor. xiii 3
cf 1 Cor. xii. 4, etc.

---

[1] Asia means, of course, the Roman province of the name, roughly the western third of what we call Asia Minor.
[2] For the post-classical use of *alias* = *aliter*, see *Thesaurus* s.v., and Hoppe, pp. 110 f
[3] For the hypallage here, see Hoppe, p. 87.
[4] The bishop referred to was either Victor (so Allix, Oehler) or his predecessor Eleutherus (so Blondel, Neander) For the traditional lists of these bishops see C. H. Turner in *Journ Theol Studies*, vol. xviii. pp 108, 118 The date of Victor's accession is put at M. Aurelius XVII (= A.D 163), cf. Turner, p. 115, but the true date appears to be 189. Montanus founded Montanism in Phrygia about the middle of the second century Prisca and Maximilla were women followers of his. All prophesied and maintained the superiority of spiritual gifts over official position in the Church. See d'Alès, chap. ix.

was seeking to introduce peace to the churches of Asia and Phrygia, it was he who did, by making false statements about these very prophets and their churches, and by defending the authoritative acts of his predecessors, compel him both to recall the letters of peace that had been already despatched and to give up his project of welcoming their gifts. So Praxeas managed two pieces of the devil's business at Rome, he drove out prophecy and brought in heresy, he put the Paraclete[1] to flight and crucified the Father. Praxeas' "tares" have borne fruit here too, having been "sown above" the pure teaching "while" many "slept"; thereafter through him whom God willed,[2] they seemed to have been revealed and even pulled up by the roots.[3] Furthermore, the presbyter[4] who taught them had given sureties for his reform, and his signed promise remains in the possession of the carnal men in whose presence the transaction took place at the time. Ever since there has been silence. As for ourselves, the recognition and defence of the Paraclete afterwards separated us from these carnal men.[5] Those tares[6] had, however,

cf. Matt xiii. 25 etc.

[1] Remember that Montanus accepted the title of "the Paraclete" (Euseb., *Hist. Eccl.*, v 14)

[2] *I. e.* probably a reference to Tertullian himself.

[3] For *traductae* thus used cf. Lofstedt, *Krit. Bemerkungen zu Tertullian's Apologeticum* (Lund, 1918), p. 72.

[4] Reading with Turner *presbiter istorum* there is no adverb *pristinum*. Yet Hoppe, p 18, explains *pristinum doctor* as = *qui pristinum docet*.

[5] The "carnal" men (*psychici*) are the Catholics, as opposed to the Montanists, who are spiritual. Cf. d'Alès, pp. 453 f.

[6] For the similes of Tertullian, see Hoppe, pp 193–220 (this one, p. 197).

28   TERTULLIAN AGAINST PRAXEAS   [1, 2

cf. Matt. at that time everywhere "choked" the seed. For
xiii. 7 some time that fact lay hidden through hypocrisy,
such was its cunning vitality, and now it has burst
forth again. But it will also be again uprooted;
if the Lord wills, in this present age;[1] but if
cf. Matt not, "at their proper season" all the corrupt crops
xiii 30 "will be gathered together," and "along with all
cf. Matt.
xiii. 40, 41 other stumbling-blocks" will "be burnt by un-
cf. Matt.
iii. 12 quenchable fire."[2]

2. Therefore after a time the Father that was
born and the Father that suffered, God Himself
cf various the "all-powerful" Lord is preached as Jesus
creeds Christ. But we both always and now more than
before,[3] as being better instructed by "the Para-
cf John clete," "who" of course "leads us into all truth,"
xvi 13
cf. Nicene "believe" indeed "in one God," but subject to
Creed this arrangement, which we call economy, that to
the one God there should also belong a Son, His
own Word, who has come forth from Him,
John i. 3 "through Whom all things were made, and without Whom nothing was made"[4]; that it was He
cf. various who was put by the Father into "the virgin," and
creeds "born from" her, both man and God, son of man
cf Matt. and Son of God, and surnamed "Jesus Christ",
i 16

[1] For this sense of *commeatus*, see the *Thesaurus* s.v., Hoppe,
p 120, d'Alès, p 68
[2] For other examples of the ending $\smile\smile\smile\smile\smile\smile$, see Hoppe,
pp 155 f.
[3] On the relation of this passage to the official creed of the churches
of North Africa, see the important section in d'Alès, pp. 254–261
[4] The invariable, or almost invariable, punctuation of this verse
down to the latter part of the fourth century see the evidence set
forth in my critical apparatus to *Novum Testamentum Graece*, and
add W (the Freer-Washington codex) to the uncials there cited.

that it was He "who suffered, died, and was buried" "according to the Scriptures," and was raised again by the Father, and being taken back "into heaven¹ is seated at the right hand of the Father, and will come to judge the living and the dead"; who afterwards, according to His promise, sent from the Father the Holy "Spirit,² the Paraclete," the sanctifier of the faith of them who believe in the Father and the Son and the Holy Spirit. That this rule (of faith) has run its course from the beginning of the Gospel, even before the days of all the earlier heretics, and much more before the days of Praxeas, who is but of yesterday, will be proved as much by the very succession of all the heretics as it will be by the very modernity of the Praxeas of yesterday. Just as was done in exactly the same way "against all heresies,"³ so let us from the present case also derive the preliminary judgment that whatsoever is first is true, while whatsoever is later is corrupt But without prejudice, however, to this "preliminary declaration,"⁴

cf various creeds
cf 1 Cor. xv 3, 4
cf various creeds

cf John xiv 16

cf Tert. praescr haer 31

Ibid

---

¹ For the abl *caelo* = acc *caelum*, see Hoppe, pp 40 f
² It is surely not fanciful to suppose that in what has just preceded Tertullian has had some creed in view He quotes in a fuller form than the Apostles' Creed, and curiously anticipates certain later forms The reader should consult Dr Sanday in *Journal of Theological Studies*, vol 1, pp 3 ff "Recent Research on the Origin of the Creed"
³ This must be a reference, as C H Turner points out, to the passage in the *De praescriptione haereticorum* "ex ipso ordine manifestatur id esse dominicum et uerum quod sit prius traditum, id autem extraneum et falsum quod sit posterius immissum"
⁴ The word *praescriptio* is borrowed from Law, where it means "a preliminary declaration, by which one cuts the arguments of the opposite party short" (d'Alès, p 201).

room for revision of judgment[1] must also be everywhere given, for the instruction and fortification of certain people, if only to prevent each single perversity from the appearance of condemnation, not after, but before it has been judged. And this applies especially to the perversity that thinks it possesses the undiluted truth, in holding the view that it must not believe in one God in any other way than by saying that this selfsame God is both Father and Son and Spirit. As if by parity of reasoning one of these were not all, since all come from one, of course through unity of nature, and as if, nevertheless, the mystery[2] of the economy were maintained. This economy arranges unity in trinity, regulating three, Father, Son and Spirit—three, however, not in unchangeable condition, but in rank; not in substance, but in attitude; not in office, but in appearance,[3]—but of one nature[4] and of one reality and of one power, because there is one God from whom these ranks and attitudes and appearances are derived in the name of Father and Son and Holy Spirit. How they are subject[5] to

---

[1] Hoppe, p. 138 n., classes the meanings of *retractatus* in Tertullian

[2] On the word *sacramentum* in Tertullian there has been much discussion: see d'Alès, pp 321 ff.

[3] This clause appears to indicate an unequal share of divinity between the Three.

[4] The word *substantia* (= nature) recurs cc 5, 8, 12, 26, 27: see Dean Strong in *Journal Theol. Studies*, vol. iii pp. 38-40, Dr. J. F Bethune-Baker, *ibid*, vol. iv. pp 440-442, both cited by d'Alès, p 81, n 2, who in n. 3 defines *status* in Tertullian as "*nature* ou *réalité*."

[5] For the indicative in indirect questions, see Hoppe, p. 72.

number and are yet not divided, these expositions will make clear as they advance.

3. All simple people, not to say the unwise and unprofessional[1] (who always constitute the majority of believers), since even the rule of faith[2] itself removes them from the plurality of "the gods" of this world to "the one true God," become greatly terrified through their failure to understand that, while He must be believed to be one, it is along with His economy, because they judge that economy, implying a number and arrangement of trinity, is really a division[3] of unity, whereas[4] unity, deriving trinity from itself, is not destroyed by it, but made serviceable. Therefore they now circulate the statement that two and three are preached by us, while they judge that they are worshippers of one God, just as if the irrational contraction of unity did not produce heresy and the rational expansion of trinity did not establish truth. "We hold to monarchy," they say, and even Latins, even artisans,[5] give such character to the word itself with their voices, that you might suppose they understand "monarchy" as well as they articulate the word. But the Latins are

cf 1 Cor viii. 5
cf. John xvii. 3

---

[1] "Unprofessional": possibly "uninitiated" would be better.
[2] *Regula fidei*, a regular expression in the early writers for the official creed.
[3] Hoppe (p. 168) takes *dispositionem* and *diuisionem* as an instance of alliteration, a rhetorical device.
[4] For this sense of *quando*, see Hoppe, pp. 78 f.
[5] *Etiam opifices* with Rigalt and C. H. Turner, for the impossible *et tam opifice* of MSS and editors.

anxious to preach[1] "monarchy," while even the Greeks are unwilling to understand "economy." But I, if I have culled any knowledge of both languages, know that "monarchy" means nothing else but the rule of one single person; but that monarchy, nevertheless, does not for the reason that it belongs to one, lay it down that he to whom it belongs should either not have a son or should have made his very self into a son for himself, or should not manage his monarchy through whom he will. Further I affirm that no sovranty belongs so to one in himself, is so individual, is so much monarchy, that it cannot also be administered through other agents[2] in contact with it, whom it has itself looked out to perform services for itself. If, moreover, he to whom the monarchy belongs, has also had a son, you would not at once say that it was divided and ceased to be a monarchy, if the son also were taken to share in it, but that it was just as before chiefly his by whom it is shared with his son, and while it is his, it is just as much monarchy, since it is held together by two who are so united. Therefore, if the divine monarchy also is administered by so many "legions" and armies "of angels," as it is written: "a hundred thousand times a hundred thousand were standing by Him, and a thousand times a hundred thousand were

cf Matt. xxvi 53
Dan. vii 10

---

[1] *Sonare = praedicare, significare*, is for the most part post-classical (Hoppe, p 15).
[2] "Agents" *Personas* in theology seems to be derived from *personas* in law, where *persona* has the meaning "civil personality."

in attendance upon Him," and if it did not therefore cease to belong to one, so as to cease to be a monarchy, because its affairs are managed by so many thousands of powers, what sort of an idea is it that God should seem to suffer division and dispersal[1] in the Son and in the Holy Spirit, who have obtained respectively the second and the third place, and who are such partners in the Father's substance, a division and dispersal which He does not suffer in the angels who are so many in number, who are moreover no part of the Father's substance! Do you consider that the parts and pledges and tools and the very power and the whole origin of monarchy are its undoing? That is wrong. I would rather you schooled yourself to understand the thing than to utter the word The undoing of monarchy you must understand to take place when another sovranty is superimposed on its circumstances and its own special condition, and thus becomes hostile. When another god is introduced against the Creator, then is it evil, when it leads to the dethronement of the Creator, when a number are introduced, as by the Valentini and Prodici,[2] then it leads to the overturning of monarchy; (4) but how can I who

---

[1] For many such examples of time as *diuisionem et dispersionem* in Tertullian, see Hoppe, pp 162 ff (especially p 163)

[2] That is, people like Valentinus and Prodicus, the Greek Gnostics The former was an Egyptian Greek who lived from about A D 135 to A D 160 in Rome Prodicus was less important, and of him little or nothing is known Their doctrine set forth a plurality of divinities (Cf Irenaeus *passim*, and Tertullian, *Aduersus Valentinianos.*)

derive the Son from nowhere else, but from the substance of the Father, "doing" nothing without "the" Father's "will," obtaining "all power" from the Father, how can I be supposed[1] to be breaking up monarchy, which, as handed over by the Father to the Son, I preserve in the Son? May I say this too with regard to the third grade, that I do not regard "the Spirit as coming" from anywhere else than "from the Father" through the Son.[2] Beware then lest it be rather you who are breaking up monarchy, in overturning its arrangement and management,[3] established as they are in as many names as God willed. To such a degree, moreover, does it remain in its established condition, though trinity be introduced, that it has even to be restored to the Father by the Son, even as the Apostle writes about the final end "When He has handed over the kingdom to His God and Father. For He must reign till God put His enemies under His feet,"—of course according to the psalm: "Sit at my right hand, till I make thine enemies a footstool to thy feet"—"when, moreover, all things are subjected to him save Him who subjected all things unto Him, then He Himself also will be subjected unto Him who subjected all

cf. John vi 38
cf. John xvii 2

cf John xv. 26

1 Cor. xv 24, 25

Ps. cix. 1
1 Cor. xv 26, 27

---

[1] Reading with C H Turner *uideri* for *de fide* of MSS and edd. *De fide*, however, might conceivably mean "from the vantage ground of faith"

[2] Note this careful statement, taken perhaps from the Greeks (cf. d'Alès, p 96) The first definite statement in a creed of Procession of the Spirit from the Son as well as the Father is in the Fourth Council of Toledo (A D 589)

[3] Note this case of rime. cf. Hoppe, p. 163.

things unto Him, that God may be all things in all." We see therefore that monarchy is not harmed although it be to-day with the Son, because it is both in its established condition with the Son and along with its established condition it will be restored to the Father by the Son. So no one will break it up in this way, that is, by admitting the Son, to whom it is well known that it was handed over by the Father and by whom it is well known it will one day be restored to the Father. By this one passage[1] of the Apostle's letter we have already been able to show[2] that the Father and the Son are two, because, apart from the fact of the names Father and Son, there is the other fact that He who "handed over the kingdom" and He to whom it was handed over, and likewise "He who subjected" and He to whom He was subjected, are of necessity two.[3] *cf. 1 Cor. xv 24* *cf. 1 Cor. xv. 28*

5. But because they make out that the two are one, so that the Father and Son are regarded as the same, we must weigh also the whole subject of the Son, whether He exists and who He is and how He comes to be, and thus the fact itself will vindicate its outward expression which protects the Scriptures and their translations. Some say that even Genesis in the Hebrew begins thus: "In the beginning God *cf. Gen. 1. 1*

---

[1] *Capitulum* indicates a section, usually longer than a modern verse, but considerably shorter than a modern chapter

[2] For *ostendisse = ostendere*, see Hoppe, pp. 52–54, who furnishes many parallels

[3] If we assume synaloepha, as Hoppe does (p. 154 n. 3), this is an instance of the commonest type of ending in Tertullian ($- \smile - \smile$).

made for Himself a Son."[1] That this is not reliable I am induced to believe by other arguments drawn from God's arrangement itself which He followed from "before the foundation of the world" down to the begetting of a Son.[2] For at the first God was alone, He was to Himself both universe and place and everything, alone, moreover, because there was nothing outside but Himself.[3] But even at that time He was not alone; for He had with Him what He had in Himself, namely, His reason. For God is rational, and reason was first in Him, and thus it is that from Him it comes into all things.[4] This reason is His own thought; this is what the Greeks call "Logos," which word we translate also by "speech," and therefore it is now our (Latin) custom by a simple translation to declare that "the Word was in the beginning with God," although it is more fitting that reason should be regarded as the older, because a God rational even before the beginning is not from the beginning given to speech,[5] and because even speech itself, since it depends on reason, shows that the latter is earlier, as being its foundation. Yet for all that there is no difference. For

cf. John xvii. 24, etc.

John i. 1

John i. 2

---

[1] Oehler compares Hil in Ps ii 2, Hier Quaest. Hebr in Gen. tom II p 507, ed Bened

[2] The teaching here is derived from the Greek Apologists the parallels are set out in detail by d'Alès, pp 86 f

[3] For a Hippolytean parallel, see d'Alès, p 89

[4] Reading *in omnia* with C H Turner, for *omnia* of MSS and edd

[5] The word *sermonalis* appears to be a coinage of Tertullian to correspond with *rationalis* (Hoppe, p. 116). Note the rime between the two (Hoppe, p 166).

although God "had" not yet "uttered His word," Ps cvi 20
all the same He had it both with and in reason
itself within Himself, while silently meditating and
arranging with Himself what He was afterwards to
state in word. For meditating and arranging in
company with His reason, He made that into word
which He was dealing with by word. To understand it more easily, take knowledge from yourself,
I pray you, as from "the image and likeness" of cf Gen. 1.
God, that you also have in yourself reason, being a 26
rational living being, not only made as you are,
of course by a rational Creator, but also given life cf. Gen. ii.
from His own nature. See, when you silently meet 7
with yourself in the process of thinking, that this
very process goes on within you by reason meeting
you along with word at every movement of your
thought, at every beat of your understanding.
Whatsoever you think is word, whatsoever you
understand is speech.[1] You must speak that within
your mind, and while you speak, you experience
in conversation with you the word which contains
this very reason. By means of reason you think
in company with word, and speak, and when you
speak through word, you are thinking. So some-
how there is in you a second word, through which
you speak when meditating and through which
you meditate when speaking: the word itself is
different. With how much more completeness,

---

[1] Reading *oratio* with Kroymann, for the corruption, cf the variants in Ep Phil. iv 17, where certain Pelagian MSS. read *orationem* (cf. comment), where the Vulgate has *ratione*

cf Gen. 1 26then, does this take place in God, whose "image and likeness" you also are deemed to be![1] Since He has reason in Himself even when silent, and in having reason has word also, it may be, therefore, that I have not made a rash beginning by laying down that even then "before the foundation of the universe" God was not alone, having in Himself alike reason and word in reason, which (word) He had made second to Himself by exercising it within Himself.[2]

cf. John xvii. 24, etc.

6. This power and this arrangement of divine understanding is indicated in the Scriptures also under the name "wisdom." For what could be wiser than the reason or word of God? Therefore listen to wisdom also created as the second person: "At first the Lord created me as a beginning of ways for his works, before He made the earth, before the mountains were set; yea, before all the hills He begat me," creating and begetting me in His understanding of course. Then take knowledge of her standing by at the time when He Himself worked[3]: "When He was preparing heaven," she says, "I was present with Him at the time; and how strong He made the clouds that are overhead, above the winds, and how securely He placed the sources of that quarter which is under heaven! I was with

Prov viii 22, 23, 25

Prov viii. 27, 28, 30

---

[1] A good collection of examples of *censeri* as used by Tertullian in *Thes* s.v., also in d'Alès, pp 366 f.
[2] Observe the ending ‿ ⌣ ‿ ‿ ⌣ (without synaloepha), frequent in Tertullian (Hoppe, p 156)
[3] Read, with C H Turner, *ipsius operationi*, for *ipsa separatione* of the MSS. (*in ipsa operatione*, Kroymann).

Him constructing,[1] I it was in whom He rejoiced; and daily was I delighted before His face" Then, as soon as God had willed to put forth into His own matter and form that which He had in company with the reason and word of wisdom arranged within Himself, he first brought forth the word itself, having in itself its own inseparable reason and wisdom, that everything might be made through the very (word) by which all had been planned and arranged, or rather already made, so far as God's thought was concerned.[2] For this they still lacked: they had yet to become known and remembered before the eyes of each person in their appearances and substances.[3]

7. It is then, therefore, that even the word itself[4] takes its own appearance and vesture, namely sound and expression, when "God says: 'Let there be made light.'" This is the complete birth of the word, since it proceeds out of God. Having been first created by Him as far as thought is concerned, under the name of wisdom—"the Lord created me as a beginning of ways,"—then begotten to actuality—"when He was preparing heaven, I was with Him,"—thereafter, making as

Gen. i.

Prov. viii. 22

Prov. viii. 27

---

[1] For the periphrastic conjugation *eram conpingens*, see Hoppe, pp 59 f
[2] This passage is compared with passages from the Greek Apologists in d'Alès, pp 87 f
[3] The same metrical ending as in chapters 1, 5, and 7, etc (see Hoppe, p 156).
[4] The relation of the first part of this chapter to the Greek Apologists is set forth by d'Alès, pp 90 ff

Father[1] for Himself Him from whom He proceeds and thus becomes His Son, He was made "first-begotten," as having been begotten before everything, and "only-begotten," as having been alone begotten from God, in a real sense from the womb of His own mind, according as even the Father Himself testifies: "My mind hath given forth a good word." Rejoicing, He thereupon addresses Him, who in like manner rejoices in His presence: 'Thou art my Son, this day have I begotten thee,"[2] and "Before the morning star was, I begat thee." Even so the Son from His own person declares the Father under the name of wisdom "The Lord created me as a beginning of ways for His works, yea, before all the hills were, He begat me." And if here indeed wisdom seems to say that she was created by the Lord for His works and ways, elsewhere, however, it is shown that "all things were made through the Word, and without it was nothing made,'[3] even as again we have the words: "By His word were the heavens established, and by His spirit all their strength": by that spirit, of course, which was in the word. It is clear that it is one and the same power that passes now under the name of wisdom, now under the title "word," which received "a be-

cf. Col 1 15, etc.
cf John 1 14, etc.
Ps xliv. 2
Ps ii. 7 (Luke iii 22, etc)
Ps cix 3
Prov viii. 22, 25
John 1 3
Ps. xxxii 6
Prov viii 22

---

[1] *Patrem* d'Alès (p 90) saw that *parem* of the editions was wrong, and conjectured *patrem*, Kroymann found the latter in MSS and rightly reads it in his editions. There is no reference to equality here, but only to paternity
[2] Luke iii 22 as read by Western documents for the most part. see my apparatus to *N T Gr ad hoc*
[3] See the note on chap ii p 28.

ginning of ways for the works" of God, and which "established the heaven"—"through which all things were made, and without which nothing was made" Let us dwell no longer on this subject, as if the word itself were not meant when we find the names "wisdom," "reason," and the whole divine "mind" and "spirit," which was made the Son of God, from which he proceeded and was begotten.

"Then," you say, "you argue that the word is some material, built up of spirit and wisdom and reason?"[1] Certainly for you do not want it to be regarded as in itself material through the independence of its matter, lest it[2] might appear as a sort of object and person and, being second to God, might thus be able to make two, Father and Son, God and Word "For what," you say, "is word, but voice and a sound of the mouth, and as the school teachers teach, a striking against air, intelligible to the hearing, but something empty and vain and bodiless?'" But I say that nothing could have gone forth from God vain and empty, since the source from which it is brought is neither vain nor empty, and that what came forth from so great a material and made such great materials, cannot be immaterial; for He it was who also made what was made through Him. What sort of a notion is it that He "without Whom nothing was made," should Himself be nothing, that an

Ps xxxii 6
John 1 3

cf Donatus I 1, etc

---

[1] The true readings were pointed out by C H Turner, namely *sophia et ratione* (instead of *sophiae traditione*) and *haberi in se* (for *habere in re*)

[2] Read *ne ut* with Kroymann for MSS *ut* simply

unsubstantial person should have worked what was solid, an empty person what was full, an incorporeal person what was corporeal! For although sometimes a thing can come into being different from that through which it comes into being, yet nothing can come into being through that which is empty and vain. Is the word of God an empty and shadowy thing which was called the Son? which was sur-named God Himself? "And the Word was with God, and the Word was God." It is written. "Thou shalt not take the name of God in vain." That is assuredly He who "being in the image of God thought it not robbery to be equal to God." In what image of God? Assuredly in some image, not in none at all. For who will deny that God is body,[1] even though "God is spirit"? For spirit is a particular kind of body in its own image But if even those "invisible things," whatsoever they are, have with God both their body and their shape, by means of which they are visible to God alone, how much more will that which has been put forth from His own being, have being?[2] For whatsoever the being of the Word was, I call it a person and I claim the name "Son" for Him, and in recognising Him as Son, I claim that He is second to the Father.[3]

John i 1

Exod. xx. 7 (cf Deut v 11) Phil. ii. 6

John iv 24

cf Rom i. 20 (?)

---

[1] "Body," render perhaps rather by "substance" passages illustrating the uses of this word in Tertullian are given by d'Alès, p 62

[2] This thought is paralleled in the early Greek Apologists: see the evidence in d'Alès, p 92 The sentence is explained in some detail by Dr J F. Bethune-Baker in *Journ Theol Studies*, vol. iv pp 441 f

[3] See the note at the end of chap 6.

8. If any one thinks that herein I am introducing some *probolé*,[1] that is, projection of one thing from another, as Valentinus[2] does, when he brings forth from an Aeon one and another Aeon, in the first place I will tell you this: truth does not refrain from using this word and the thing and the origin it represents, for the reason that heresy also uses it · nay rather heresy got from the truth the materials for constructing its own falsehood. Was the word of God brought forth or not? Here plant your step with me.[3] If it was brought forth, learn of the projection belonging to the truth, and it is heresy's look out if it has imitated anything from the truth. Our present question is who uses a certain thing[4] and how he uses it and the word describing it. Valentinus distinguishes and separates his projections from the Creator, and places them so far from Him, that the Aeon does not know the Father; for he longs to know Him, and cannot, nay he is almost swallowed and broken up into the remaining material. But amongst us it is only "the Son that knows the Father," and He Himself "has revealed the bosom of the Father" and "He has heard" and "seen" all things with the Father and "what things He was

cf Matt. xi. 27, etc. John i 18
cf John xv 15
cf John v. 19

---

[1] For *prolatio* as a Latin rendering of Greek *probolé*, see Hoppe, p 123, n 1

[2] Valentinus, the Gnostic: see the note on chap 3 fin The doctrine of Aeons was one of the most characteristic parts of the Gnostic system

[3] Other examples of the metaphor *gradum figere* in Hoppe, p 208, n 1.

[4] For the two question clauses without connective, a Latin and Greek idiom, cf Hoppe, p 74

commanded by the Father, these He also speaks"; and it was "not His own will, but" the Father's that He accomplished, that will which He knew at close quarters, nay from His inmost soul. "For who knows what is in God but the Spirit who is in Himself?" The word, moreover, is equipped[1] with the spirit, and if I may say so, the word's body is spirit.[2] The word, therefore, was both always in the Father, even as He says. "I in the Father," and always with God, as it is written: "And the Word was with God," and never separated from the Father or different[3] from the Father, because: "I and the Father are one." This will be the projection of truth, the guardian of unity, by which we say that the Son was brought forth from the Father, but not separated. For God brought forth the Word, even as the Paraclete also teaches, as the root does the shrub, the source the river, and the sun the ray. For these forms too are projections of the natures from which they proceed. Nor should I hesitate to call the Son both the shrub of the root and the river of the source and the ray of the sun, because every origin is a parent,[4] and all that is brought forth from the origin is offspring, much more the Word of God, which also in a real sense received the name of Son. And yet the shrub is not distinguished from

---

[1] For *structus = instructus*, cf Hoppe, pp 138 f.
[2] With this passage d'Alès, p 86, compares passages in the Greek Apologists
[3] For the *a (ab)* after *alius*, cf chaps 9 (*quater*), 18 (Hoppe, p 36)
[4] D'Alès, p 92, compares this passage with some in the Greek Apologists

the root, nor the river from the source, nor the ray from the sun, even as the Word is not distinguished from God either. Therefore according to the pattern of these examples I declare that I speak of two, God and His Word, the Father and His Son. The root and the shrub are also two things, but joined together; the source and the river are two forms, but undivided; the sun and the ray are two forms, but they cleave together. Everything that proceeds from something, must be second to that from which it proceeds, but it is not therefore separated. Where, however, there is a second, there are two, and where there is a third, there are three. The Spirit is third with respect to God and the Son, even as the fruit from the shrub is third from the root, and the channel from the river is third from the source, and the point[1] where the ray strikes something is third[2] from the sun. Yet in no respect is it banished from the original source from which it derives its special qualities. Thus the Trinity running down from the Father through stages linked and united together,[3] offers no obstacle to monarchy and conserves the established position of the economy.[4]

[1] My rendering of *apex* is cumbrous: Blunt, *Right Use*, etc, p 504, renders by "sparkle," Kaye, *Eccles. Hist* (cheap edition), pp 265 f, by "terminating point"
[2] The repetition of the word *tertius* (anaphora) is a rhetorical device used for effect: cf Hoppe, pp. 146 f
[3] The alliteration *consertos conexos* is an intentional rhetorical device: Hoppe, pp 148 ff
[4] This ending ($-\smile-\ -\smile\smile$) is one of the rarer types in Tertullian, occurring in about thirteen per cent. of the cases only (Hoppe, pp. 156 f.)

9. Everywhere remember that I have announced this rule by which I testify that Father and Son and Spirit are unseparated from one another, and thus you will recognise what is meant and how it is meant.[1] Understand then ; I say that the Father is one, the Son another, and the Spirit another—every untrained or perverse person takes this saying wrongly, as if it expressed[2] difference, and as the result of difference meant a separation of Father, Son and Holy Spirit, but it is of necessity that I say this, when they contend that Father, Son and Spirit are the same person, fawning on monarchy at the expense of economy —but that it is not by difference that the Son is other[3] than the Father, but by distribution, and it is not by division that He is other, but by distinction, because Father and Son are not the same, being different one from the other even in measure. For the Father is all being, but the Son is a tributary of the whole and a portion, as He Himself declares: "Because the Father is greater than I." In the psalm He is sung of as being "made" by Him "a little lower than the angels"[4] So also the Father is other than the Son, since He is greater than the Son, since it is one that begets,

John xiv. 28

cf. Ps. viii 6 (Heb ii 7)

---

[1] For the double question, without connective, cf. Hoppe, p 74.
[2] *sonet = significet* (Hoppe, p 15).
[3] For *alius, a,* here and thrice below in this chapter, cf Hoppe, p. 36
[4] Cf. cc 14, 26, which like this passage favour subordinationism ; but the passages must be read in conjunction with others of contrary tendency in cc. 9, 11 (cf d'Alès, pp. 100 f.).

another that is begotten, since it is one that sends, another that is sent; since it is one that acts, another through whom action takes place. It is well that the Lord also, using this word in reference to the person of the Paraclete, indicated not division, but arrangement; for, He said: "I will ask the Father, and He will send you 'another' advocate, the Spirit of reality," meaning a Paraclete other than Himself in the same way as we also mean a Son other than the Father,[1] to show the third stage in the Paraclete, as we show the second in the Son because of our regard to economy. Does not the very fact that Father and Son are named, mean that the one thing is different from the other? For certainly all things will be what they are called, and what they shall be, *that* they will be called, and the difference in the names cannot be at all mixed up, any more than the difference in the objects they will represent. "Yea, yea, nay, nay, for what is more than 'yea' and 'nay' is from the evil one." 10. So both the Father "is" and the Son "is"[2] (just as day is and night is); and neither is day the same as night, nor Father the same as Son. If they were, both would be one and either of the two would be both, as these foolish Monarchians make out.

John xiv. 16

Matt v 37

"He Himself," they say, "made Himself Son

---

[1] For the omission of *dicit* and *dicimus*, cf Hoppe, p. 145
[2] Here C H Turner is followed as to arrangement, reading and translation: *ita et pater et filius "est."*

for Himself." Nay, rather a father makes a son and a son a father,[1] and those who come from one or other, cannot in any way be made by themselves for themselves, so that a father should make himself a son for himself and a son should offer himself as a father to himself. What God created, God Himself also maintains. A father must needs have a son, to be a father, and a son must have a father, to be a son. It is one thing to have, another to be. For example, to be a husband I must have a wife, I shall not be myself a wife to myself. So also to be a father, I must have had a son, I myself shall not be a son to myself, and to be a son, I shall have a father; I myself shall not be a father to myself. If I have what makes me so, then I shall be so; a father, if I have a son, a son, if I have a father. Further, if I shall myself be any of those, I no longer have that which I shall myself be; neither a father, because I shall myself be a father, nor a son, because I shall myself be a son. In so far as I must have one of those two, and be the other, just in so far, if I am both, I shall not be one of the two, as long as I do not possess the other. For if I myself shall be a son, who am also a father, I no longer have a son, but I am myself a son. But if I have not a son, while I am myself a son, how shall I be a father? For I must have a son to be a father. I am therefore not a son because I have not a father, who makes a son. Equally if I myself am a father, who am

---

[1] This sentence supports the new reading *patrem* in c 7

also a son, I no longer have a father, but I am myself a father. But if I have not a father, while I am myself a father, how shall I be a son? For I must have a father, to be a son. I shall therefore not be a father, because I have not a son, who makes one a father. This will all be a contrivance of the devil to shut out the one from the other, while by enclosing both in one under the support he gives to monarchy, he causes neither to be possessed, so that he should not be a father who of course has not a son, nor should he be a son who equally has not a father, for while he is a father, he will not be a son. So do they hold to monarchy, who hold together at the same time neither Father nor Son. But "nothing is difficult to" God who does not know it? and, "what is impossible with the world is possible with God" who is ignorant of this? and "God chose the foolish things of the world to put the wise things to confusion" we read all this in Scripture. "Therefore," they say, "it was 'not difficult for' God to make Himself both Father and Son against the law handed down to human circumstances. For it was 'not difficult for' God either that 'a barren woman should bear' contrary to nature, or that 'a virgin' either should do so." Clearly, "nothing is difficult to" God, but if we take such inconsiderate advantage of this thought in our assumptions, we shall be able to imagine anything we like about God, as if He acted simply because He had the power to act. But we are not to believe that because "He can do all things," therefore He did even what He did not do, but we must ask whether He did it.¹ He could, if He had wished, have provided² man with wings to fly, as He did for kites; nevertheless He did not at once proceed to do it simply because it was in His power. He could have at once put to death² both Praxeas and all other heretics alike; yet simply because He had the power He did not do so. For "it was meet that there should be" both kites³ and "heretics," it was also meet that the Father should be crucified! In this way there will be something even "difficult to" God, namely, whatsoever He has not done, not because He could not, but because He willed not. For God's power is His will, and His inability is His unwillingness. What He willed, He was both able and ready to do. Therefore—because, if He willed to make Himself into a son for Himself, He could have done it, and because if He could, He did it—you will prove that He both could and willed, if once you prove that He did it.

cf. Sap xi 23

cf 1 Cor xi. 19

cf Job xlii. 2

11. You will have to prove as clearly from the Scriptures as we prove it, that He made His word a son for Himself. For if He names His Son (and there will be no Son other than He who came forth from Himself, but the Word proceeded from

---

¹ Note the reasonableness of the view just expressed; cf. d'Alès, pp 35, 66.
² For the perfect infinitive after *posse*, where the present infinitive would be expected, cf. Hoppe, p 53.
³ For the comparison with kites here, see Hoppe, p. 199

Himself), that will be the Son, not Himself, from whom He proceeded. For He did not Himself proceed from Himself. Moreover, you who say that the Father and the Son are the same, argue that the same both brought forth and proceeded from Himself. Though God could have done[1] this, yet He did not do it. Or set forth the proof I demand, like my own, that is that the Scriptures indicate the same to be Son and Father in the same way as with us the Father and Son are indicated differentially, differentially, I say, not separately. Just as I produce God's saying: "my mind has given forth a good word," do you retort with the statement that God has somewhere said. "my mind has given forth myself, a good word," so that it should be Himself who both gave forth and was that which He gave forth, and Himself who brought forth and who was brought forth, if He Himself is both Word and God. Again: I point out that the Father said to the Son: "Thou art my Son, this day have I begotten thee." If you should want me to believe that the Father Himself is also the Son, show me this declaration elsewhere. "The Lord said to Himself: I am my son, I have this day begotten myself"; in like manner also: "Before the morning star I begat myself"; and: "I the Lord created myself as a beginning of ways for my works, yea, before any of the hills were, I begat myself," and any other

Ps xliv. 2

cf Ps xliv 2

Ps ii 7 (Luke iii. 22)

cf Ps. ii. 7 (Luke iii 22)

cf Ps. cix. 3

cf. Prov. viii 22, 25

---

[1] For the perfect infinitive after *posse* = present infinitive, cf Hoppe, p. 53.

passages after this likeness. Whom was God, the Lord of all things, afraid thus to proclaim, if such was the fact? Was He afraid He should not be believed, if He declared Himself in plain language to be both Father and Son? Nay: one thing, however, He did fear, falsehood—being afraid of Himself and His own truth;[1] and therefore believing God truthful I know that He has not declared differently from what He arranged, and has not arranged differently from what He declared. But you would make Him untruthful and false, and a deceiver of these believers,[2] if, although Himself a son to Himself, he gave to another the person of His Son, since[3] all the Scriptures make the Trinity clear and the distinction within it, from which Scriptures our objection is also taken, namely that He who speaks and He about whom He speaks and He to whom He speaks, cannot be regarded as one and the same, because neither perversity nor deception befits God, that although it was Himself to whom He was speaking, He should be speaking rather to another, and not to Himself. Listen, therefore, also to other words of the Father touching the Son, spoken through the medium of Isaiah:

Isa xlii 1 "Behold my Son whom I have chosen, my beloved, in whom I am well pleased, I will put my spirit

---

[1] C H. Turner's view merits mention, and may be right He reads *ueritatis auctorem* for *ueritus autem* "one thing nevertheless he did fear, that the Author of Truth should falsify himself and his truth"

[2] *Fides* (abstract) = *fideles* (concrete). cf Hoppe, p 93, who gives parallels.

[3] For *quando* = "since," cf. Hoppe, p 78.

upon Him, and He will preach judgment to the nations" Take this also addressed to Himself "It is a great thing for thee, that thou shouldest be called my son to raise up the tribes of Jacob and to turn back the scattering of Israel, I have set thee as a light to the nations, that thou mayest be salvation to the ends of the earth." Take now also words of the Son touching the Father: "The Spirit of the Lord is upon me, wherefore He hath anointed me to give the good news unto men." Likewise to the Father in the psalm: "Lord God, forsake me not, till I preach of thine arm to all that shall be born"; likewise in another "Lord, wherefore are they multiplied that seek to crush me?" But almost all the psalms look forward to Christ's person, and set forth[1] the Son speaking to the Father, that is, Christ to God Observe also the Spirit speaking as the third person about the Father and the Son. "The Lord said unto my Lord · Sit on my right hand, till I make thine enemies a footstool to thy feet." Likewise through Isaiah "Thus saith the Lord to my Lord the Anointed " likewise through the same to the Father regarding the Son · "Lord, who hath believed our report, and to whom hath the arm of the Lord been revealed? We have preached about him: even as a young boy, even as a root in thirsty ground, and he had no beauty nor glory." These

margin references: Isa xlix 6; Luke iv 18 (cf. Isa lxi. 1); Ps lxx 18; Ps. iii.; Ps cix. 1; Isa xlv 1; Isa liii. 1–2

---

[1] The fullest discussion of the word *repraesentare* is in d'Alès pp 356–360. Cf also Prof H B Swete in *Journ Theol. Stud.* III., pp. 161–177. It is used in a *moral* sense here.

are but few passages out of many. For we are not striving to go through all the passages of Scripture, since by calling in the testimony of the full majesty and authority in individual passages, we find greater opportunity for attack in reviewing them[1] By these passages, therefore, few as they are, the distinction within the Trinity is yet clearly set forth: for there is He who declares, the Spirit, and the Father to whom He declares, and the Son about whom He declares. So also with all other things that are uttered now by the Father about the Son[2] or to the Son, now by the Son about the Father or to the Father, now by the Spirit · they establish each person in His own proper self.[3]

12. If you still find the number of the Trinity a stumbling-block, as if it were not knit together in a single unity, I ask you . how is it that one individual speaks in the plural: "Let *us* make man in *our* image and likeness," when He ought to have said :[4] "Let me make man in my image and likeness," inasmuch as[5] He is one individual ? But also in .what follows · "Behold, Adam was made like one of *us*," He is either deceiving or making fun of us, speaking as if He were a number, when He is one and alone and individual. Or

---

[1] For the senses of *retractatus* in Tertullian see Hoppe, p. 138, n 1

[2] Reading, with C H Turner, *a patre de filio uel ad filium, nunc a filio de patre uel ad patrem, nunc a spiritu*.

[3] For the rare ending ($-\cup-\cup\cup-$), see Hoppe, p 157.

[4] For the perfect infinitive here, where present infinitive would be expected, cf Hoppe, p 54

[5] *Utpote* should be read · *utpute* (Kroymann) is a vox nihili, being a cross between *utputa* and *utpote*, not uncommon in MSS.

was He addressing the angels, as the Jews understand, because they too fail to recognise the Son? Or was it because He was Himself Father, Son, Spirit, that for that reason, showing Himself to be plural, He spoke in a plural way to Himself? Nay, it was because the Son, the second person, His own Word, was already cleaving to Him, and the third,[1] the Spirit in the Word, that for that reason He made the announcement in the plural· "Let us make" and "ours" and "us." For He was speaking to those in conjunction with whom He was making man and in whose likeness He was making him—with the Son on the one hand, who was to put on "man," with the Spirit, on the other hand, who was to hallow man—as with servants and eyewitnesses, in accordance with the unity of the Trinity. For the following passage of Scripture distinguishes between the persons "God made man, in the image of God He made him." Why not "His own" (image), if there was one who made, and there was no one in whose image to make him? But there was One in whose image He made him, namely the Son, who, destined to be a surer and truer man, had caused His image to be called man, who then was to be "formed" out of "mud," "the image and likeness" of reality. But even in the case of the preceding works of the universe how is it written? At first, while as yet the Son did not show

Gen 1 26; iii 22

cf. Phil ii. 7, etc.

Gen. 1 27

cf. Gen. ii.
cf Gen. 1. 26

---

[1] There is something of a confusion here with regard to the three Persons, such as occurs in other writers also (cf. d'Alès, p 96)

Gen 1 3	Himself "And God said, 'Let there be light,' and it was made" immediately the Word Himself, "the
John 1 9	true light that comes[1] into the world and lightens
cf. John 1. 4	every man," and through Him "the light" of the universe also. Thereafter, too, in the Word Christ, standing by Him and carrying out His behests,[2] God willed creation, and God created:
Gen. 1 6 7	"And God said: 'Let there be a firmament,' and
Gen 1 14, 16	God made a firmament"; "and God said: 'Let there be lights,' and God made a greater and a less light." But the rest also were of course made by the same power as made what went before, namely
John 1 3	by the Word of God, "through whom all things were made and without whom nothing was made."
John 1. 1	If he was God Himself (according to John: "The Word was God"), you have two, one saying it should be done, the other doing it.[3] And how you ought to regard "the other," I have already declared, "other" in respect of rôle, not of nature;[4] by way of distinction, not of division. But although I hold,[5] everywhere to one being in three

---

[1] The true Cyprianic reading, as Turner points out, is *ueniens*, ι e ἐρχόμενον is made to agree with φῶs Doubtless it was so taken by Tertullian also   I should also insert the *omnem* omitted by scribal inadvertence before the almost identical *hominem* The passage would then read *ipse statim sermo* "ueia lux quae nluminat omnem hominem ueniens in hunc mundum" The *mundialis lux* is the sun

[2] The alliteration *adsist. admin* is an intentional rhetorical device (Hoppe, p. 149)

[3] Perhaps *fiant* should be read for *fiat*, corresponding better to *facta sunt*

[4] On this passage see Dean Strong, *Journ Theol Stud*, III p 38.

[5] *Teneam* is potential the construction is paratactic The parallels in Hoppe, p 83, show that there is no need to insert *etsi*, as Kroymann does.

that cleave together, yet the need of expressing my meaning makes me speak of the one who orders and the one who carries out the order, as different. For besides, He would not give the order, if He Himself were to act while giving it, that it should be done by him to whom He then gave the order; He would either have given the command[1] to Himself, if He were One only, or He would have done it without command, because He would not have waited to give the command to Himself

13. "Therefore," you say, "if God spoke and God acted, if God spoke and another acted, you are proclaiming two gods." If you are so obtuse, keep your opinion for the time being, and to make you hold this opinion still more,[2] listen to the mention of two gods even in a psalm: "Thy throne, God, is for everlasting, (a rod of uprightness is) [3] the rod of Thy kingdom; Thou hast loved righteousness and hated iniquity; therefore God, Thy God, hath anointed Thee" If it is "God" he is addressing, and he says that "God has been anointed by God," here too he avows two gods. In virtue of "the rod of thy kingdom"[4] Hence it is that Isaiah also refers to the person of Christ: "And Ps xliv 7, 8

Isa xlv. 14, 15

---

[1] For *iubeo* with the dative, on the analogy of *impero*, cf. Hoppe, p 29
[2] On *adhuc* with the comparative, see Hoppe, p, 110
[3] *Uirga directionis* has doubtless been omitted by homoeoarcton.
[4] *Pro* perhaps means "instead of," "in place of" The whole phrase sounds like a gloss out of its place clearly there is a corruption of some kind,

the Seboin, lofty men, will cross to Thee and follow after Thee with hands bound, and will worship Thee, because God is in Thee; for Thou art our God, and we knew it not, the God of Israel." Here too by saying "God in Thee" and "Thou God," he sets forth two, namely, Him who was in Christ and Christ[1] himself. There is more that you will find in the Gospel so many times;

John i 1 "In the beginning was the Word,[2] and the Word was with God, and the Word was God" One who was, and another with whom He was. But I also read that the name of the Lord was used in

Ps cix 1 reference to two "The Lord said unto my Lord: 'Sit at my right hand.'" And Isaiah says this·

Isa liii 1 "Lord, who hath believed our report, and to whom hath the arm of the Lord been revealed?" For he would have said "thine arm," not "the arm of the Lord," if he had not wished the Lord the Father and the Lord the Son to be understood. Also there is the still[3] older book of

Gen. xix 24 Genesis: "And the Lord rained on Sodom and Gomorrah sulphur and fire from heaven from the Lord." Either deny that this is in the Bible, or who are you to hold the opinion that the words are not to be taken in the sense in which they are written, especially those whose meaning lies not

---

[1] Read *Christum* for *spiritum* with C H. Turner The corruption (*spm* for *xpm*) is found elsewhere also

[2] This passage is illustrated from Greek Apologists by d'Alès, pp 86 f

[3] On *adhuc* with the comparative, see Hoppe, p 110, who suggests pleonasm here.

in allegories or similitudes, but in sure and simple definitions? But if you be of the number of those who would not then endure[1] the Lord's declaring Himself the Son of God, lest they should believe Him God, recollect that He is included with them in these words. "I said 'Ye are gods and sons of the Highest,'" and: "God stood in the assembly of the gods," in order that, if Scripture did not fear to declare that men, "made sons of God by faith," gods, you may know that Scripture much more were rightly conferred upon the true and only Son of God the name both of God and of Lord.[2] "Therefore," you say, "I will challenge you to preach consistently even to-day two gods and two lords in accordance with the authority of these Scriptures" God forbid! For we who by God's grace examine both the times and the motives of the Scriptures, as pupils especially of the Paraclete, not of men, do indeed lay down two, Father and Son, and even three including the Holy Spirit—according to the method of economy which produces the number, lest, as your perversity smuggles it in, the Father Himself should be believed to have been born and suffered, which it is not allowable to believe since it has not so been recorded—yet we never with our lips utter the expressions "two gods" and "two lords," not because the Father is not God and the Son is not God and the Spirit

cf John x 33

Ps lxxxi 6 (cf John x 34)
Ps lxxxi. 1
cf John 1 12
cf Gal. iii. 26

cf John xvi. 13

---

[1] For *sustinere* with the participle, Hoppe compares the use of *anechesthai* in Greek, and gives other examples, p 58
[2] Following Turner and reading *et dei et domini nomen*.

is not God and each one of them is not God, but since in the past two gods and two lords were preached simply in order that when Christ had come, he might be recognised as God and also called Lord, because he was the Son of God and the Lord. For if there were found in the Scriptures only one being both of God and the Lord, Christ would deservedly have been refused admission to the name of God and that of Lord—for it was preached that there was "no God" and Lord "but" one—and the Father Himself would be thought "to have descended," because they read of one God and one Lord, and His whole economy would have been overshadowed, which was planned and administered as subject-matter for belief But when Christ came and we learned about Him that He Himself who had in the past caused the (plural) number, having been made second to the Father, and one of three if the Spirit be included, being also the Father, who was more fully manifested by Him, the name of God and Lord was now reduced to an unity,[1] in order that because "the nations were leaving" a multitude of "images and coming to the" one "God," there might also be established a difference between the worshippers of a single and of a multiple divinity. Besides, it was the duty of Christians, as "sons of light,"

cf Exod xx 3; Deut v 7
cf Eph. iv. 10

cf 1 Thess i 9
cf Acts xv 19, etc

John xii. 36; Eph v 8,
1 Thess v 5

[1] This, I think, is the right way to take this sentence. The scriptural language latent in it has not, I think, been hitherto pointed out This is the only passage in Tertullian where it has been suggested to take *quia* in a final sense (= *ut*) (Hoppe, p 76, n 3), the *ut* in the text being regarded as consecutive.

[13, 14] TERTULLIAN AGAINST PRAXEAS 61

"to shine" in the world, worshipping and naming "the light of the world," one God and Lord But if we had named gods and lords in virtue of that knowledge which tells us that the name of God and Lord fits Father and Son and Spirit, we should have extinguished our torches and shown cowardice also in giving our testimony, we should have found everywhere open before us an opportunity to escape this, and at once proceeded to swear by gods and lords, as certain heretics do who have a number of gods. Therefore I will not use at all the expressions "gods" or "lords," but I will follow the Apostle, and if I have to name the Father and Son together, I will call the Father "God" and name Jesus Christ "the Lord." Moreover, I shall be able to speak of Christ as God, only in the way that the same Apostle does: "From whom is Christ, who is," he says, "God over all, blessed throughout all time." For I shall also call a ray of the sun by itself "sun"; but in naming the sun whose ray it is, I shall not straightway call a ray "the sun." For I am not going to make out that there are two suns. Nevertheless, I will just as much count the sun and its ray two things and two aspects of one indivisible material, as I do God and His Word, as I do Father and Son [1]

cf Matt v 14, 16 John viii 12

Rom 1 7, etc.

Rom ix 5

14. Further, there comes to our support in

---

[1] This ending ($\doublebar \smile \doublebar \doublebar \smile \doublebar$) is one of the rarer types, occurring in about thirteen per cent of the cases, cf Hoppe, pp 156 f Note that the final syllable of *patrem* is elided

claiming two, Father and Son, the rule that defined God as invisible. For when Moses in Egypt had longed for a sight of the Lord, saying:
<small>Exod. xxxiii 13</small> "If therefore I have found grace in thine eyes, reveal Thyself unto me, that I may see Thee and
<small>Exod xxxiii 20</small> know Thee," He said· "Thou canst not see my face; for no one will see my face and live," that is: he who sees it will die. But we find that God was seen by many, and yet none of those who had seen Him, died: He had, of course, been seen as far as men's powers served, not in the fullness of His
<small>cf Gen xii 7 cf Gen xxviii 13, xxxii 30 cf Isa vi 1 cf Ezek i 1 Exod xxxiii 20 Ibid.</small> divinity. The patriarchs are related to have seen God, for example Abraham and Jacob, and the prophets, as Isaiah and Ezekiel, and yet they did not die. Therefore, either they must have died if they had seen Him—"for no one will see" God "and live"—or, if they saw God and did not die, Scripture is false in stating that God said: "If a man see my face, he shall not live." Or if Scripture does not
<small>cf John i 18, etc</small> lie, either in declaring God to be invisible, or in stating that He has been seen, it must therefore be some one else who was seen, because he who was seen, the same cannot be defined as invisible, and it will follow that we must understand the Father as invisible in virtue of the fullness of His majesty, while we recognise the Son as visible in accordance with the measure of a secondary[1] nature; just as

---

[1] "secondary," i e not inferior, but derived, deduced from the other, as an irrigation canal is "deduced" from a river. But Tertullian seems here (cf. c. 26) to come perilously near to subordinationism, cf. d'Alès, p. 101. On p 102 he gives parallels to the general argument of the chapter

we may not view the sun, so far as the sum-total of its matter in the sky is concerned, but we can bear a ray of it with our eyes, as that is only a portion toned down, projected from it on to the earth. Here some one from the opposite side [1] will seek to maintain that even the Son is invisible, like a word, like breath, and in claiming one state [2] for Father and Son, to establish that Father and Son are rather one and the same. But we have said above that Scripture supports a difference by its distinction between the visible and the invisible. They will then add this point to their reasoning, that if it was the Son who then spoke to Moses, He Himself declared His face to be visible to no one, because, of course, the invisible Father Himself was (present) under the Son's name. By this means they will have the same being regarded as both visible and invisible, even as the same is both Father and Son, since a little earlier also, before He refuses to show His face to Moses, it is written that "the Lord spoke to Moses face to face, as if one were speaking to his friend," and in like manner Jacob also says: "I have seen God face to face." "Therefore the same being is visible and invisible, and because he is both, therefore also the Father Himself is invisible, but being also the Son, He is visible." As if, indeed, the explanation of the Scripture passage we are now giving were suited

cf c 14
pr
cf Exod xxxiii 20
Exod. xxxiii 11
Gen xxxii. 30

---

[1] *ex diuerso = ex diuersa parte* Tertullian is very fond of this type of phrase, where a preposition is used with the neuter of an adjective, cf Hoppe, pp. 98 ff

[2] "one state," i e the state of invisibility.

to a Son separated from the Father in His visibility!
For we say that even the Son in His own name is
invisible to the same extent as the Word and
Spirit of God are, in virtue of the state of His
being, even now also because He is God and Word
and Spirit of God, but that He was visible before
He took flesh, in the way to which He refers in
speaking to Aaron and Miriam · "And if there be
a prophet among you, I shall be known of him in
a vision, and in a dream shall I speak to him, not
in the way" he described to " Moses : I will speak to
him mouth to mouth, in my visible form," that is,
in reality, "and not in a riddle," that is, not in
a phantom ; even as also the Apostle says "Now
we see as if by means of a mirror in a riddle, but
then face to face." Therefore, when in Moses' case
He keeps the sight of Himself and face to face converse for a future date—for this was afterwards
fulfilled in the retirement " on the mountain," since
we read in the Gospel that "Moses was seen
conversing with Him"[1]—it is clear that previously
God—that is, the Son of God—had always been
seen "in a mirror" and "riddle" and "vision" and
"dream," as much by prophets and patriarchs as
also till that time by Moses himself, and the Lord
Himself indeed perchance spoke face to face,[2] yet
not in such a way that a man might see his face,
except perhaps "in a mirror, in a riddle." For if

Numb xii 6–8

I Cor xiii 12

*cf Matt xvii 1
cf Matt xvii 3,
Mark ix 4;
Luke ix 30
cf Numb xii 8, cf.
Gen xii 7; cf Gen xxviii 13, etc.*

Numb. xii. 8

---

[1] See d'Alès, p 171, for the connexion between the Transfiguration and the promise made to Moses

[2] Kroymann's punctuation is wrong here   *si forte*, as often in Tertullian and elsewhere=*fortasse*, see Mayor, Tert *Apol* index

the Lord had spoken to Moses in such a way that even Moses knew his face at close quarters, how does he immediately and on the very spot long to see His face, which he would not *long* to see, because he had seen it? How is it that the Lord also equally declares that His face cannot be seen, which He had already shown, if He really had shown it? But what is that "face" of God, the "sight" of which is refused? If it was that which was seen—"I saw God," says Jacob, ' face to face, and my soul was saved"—that "face" must be different which, if seen, slays.[1] Or was the Son indeed seen—although " face to face," yet this very sight occurred "in vision" and "dream" and "mirror and riddle," because Word and Spirit cannot be seen except in an imaginary form—and does he mean by his "face"[2] the invisible Father? Who is the Father? Will not the Son's face be His by virtue of the authority which He obtains as begotten by the Father? Is it not fitting to use the expression about some greater being: "That man is my face," and "he countenances me"? "The Father," He says, "is greater than I." Therefore the Son's face will be the Father. For, besides, what is it the Scripture says? "The spirit of His face (*lit* mask), Christ the Lord"[3]

cf Exo l xxxiii 20

Ibid.

Gen xxxii 30

cf Gen. xii 7, xxviii 13, etc

cf Numb xii. 8

Exod xxxiii 20

John xiv. 28

Lam. iv. 20

---

[1] The sentence would gain in clearness if, with C H Turner, we inserted *uisa est, alia quae* after *facies quae*

[2] On this passage and the scriptural use of *facies* in this connexion, see Thes. vol vi (1913), p 49, ll. 26 ff

[3] The MSS must be followed here as agreeing with LXX. Kroymann alters to *spiritus* (gen.) *eius persona . persona paterni spiritus* But Tertullian's agreement with LXX in not perfect In

Therefore, if "Christ is the spirit of the Father's face," it follows that He proclaimed His own face (as the result of their unity, of course), to be that of the Spirit whose face He was, namely that of the Father. It is matter for wonder whether the Son's face can be taken as the Father, who is "His head." For "God is Christ's head."

15. If I do not succeed in explaining this part of my subject by investigations of the Old Scripture, I will take from the New Testament the confirmation of my interpretation, lest whatever I attribute to the Son, you should in like manner claim for the Father. For observe, both in the Gospels and in the Apostles[1] I find that God is visible and invisible, with a clear and personal difference between the two states. John, as it were, shouts aloud : "No one hath seen God at any time," and therefore, of course, not in the past ; for he has removed all question as to time by saying that "God has *never* been seen." And the Apostle also confirms this as regards God. "whom no human being hath seen, nor indeed can see," assuredly because he who does see Him will die. These very same Apostles testify that they "have both seen and handled" Christ. But if Christ Himself is both Father and Son, how was He both seen

1 Cor xi. 3

John i 18

Ibid

1 Tim vi 16

cf Exod xxxiii 20
cf. 1 John i. 1

---

place of *eius* (his) LXX has ἡμῶν (ours) It looks as if he had falsified the text for his own purpose   R V. "The breath of our nostrils, the anointed of the Lord " Cf d'Alès, pp 98, 237.

[1] For the terms used by Tertull an to indicate Scripture or parts of Scripture, see d'Ales, p 223 ff.

and invisible? Some opponent of ours will now [1]
argue, with the view of combining this distinction of
visible and invisible in a unity, that both statements
are correct, that He was visible indeed in the
flesh, but invisible before He became flesh, with
the result that the Father, invisible before He
became flesh, is the same as the Son who is visible
in the flesh. But if the same was invisible before
becoming flesh, how is He found to have been seen
even in the past before He became flesh? Likewise, if the same was visible after becoming flesh,
how is He even now declared invisible by the
Apostles, except because it was one who even in the
past was seen "in a riddle" and was made more Numb xii
fully visible by flesh, namely, "the Word," who $^8_{\text{John i 14}}$
"was" also "made flesh," and it was another whom
"no one ever saw," the Father, of course, whose the John i 18
Word is? For let us examine who it was the
Apostles saw. "What we have seen," says John, 1 John i. 1
"what we have heard, what we with our eyes have
seen, and our hands have handled of the Word
of life." For "the Word" "of life" "was made John i 14
flesh"—was heard and seen and handled, because
flesh—who before the Incarnation was merely
"the Word in the beginning with God" the John i. 1,
Father, not the Father with Himself.[2] For [2]
although "the Word was God," yet, because God John i. 1
springs from God, it was "with God," because in
company with the Father means "with" the

[1] For *ex diuerso*, see the note on chap. 14, p. 63 Read *nunc* for *non* of the MSS. with C. H Turner
[2] Read *semet ipsum* with C. H. Turner for *sermonem* of MSS.

Father. "And we saw His glory, as of the only begotten of the Father," assuredly the Son, of course visible, "glorified" by the invisible Father. And it was for that reason (since he had called "the Word" of God "God"), lest he should encourage the assumption of his enemies, that he claimed to have seen the Father Himself, that in order to distinguish between the invisible Father and the visible Son he adds over and above [1]. "God no one hath seen at any time." Which God? The Word? Nay · "we have seen and heard and handled of the Word of life" preceded But what God? The Father, of course, "with whom was God the Word," "the only begotten Son, who Himself declared the Father's bosom." He Himself was "both heard and seen," and lest He should be believed to be an apparition, was even "handled." Him also Paul saw, but yet he did not see the Father. "Have I not," he said, "seen Jesus?" But he also surnamed "Christ" "God" "Of whom were the fathers and from whom was Christ according to the flesh, who is over all things, God blessed for ever." He also showed that God the Son was visible, that is, "the Word" of God, because he "who was made flesh" was called Christ. But about the Father he says to Timothy "Whom no one of men hath seen, nor indeed can see," amplifying further. "Who alone hath immortality and inhabiteth unapproachable light," concerning whom

---

[1] *ex abundanti* see *Thesaurus* s. v. *abundo* and Hoppe, p 101 It is very common in Tertullian.

he had also said earlier: "And to the King of the ages, immortal, invisible, the only God," that we might also ascribe the contrary qualities to the Son Himself, mortality, accessibility, who, he testifies, "died according to the Scriptures" and "was last seen by himself," by means of "approachable" "light," of course—and yet even it neither he himself could experience without danger to his sight nor could Peter, John and James, without having to reckon the chance of loss of reason, who, if they had seen, not the glory of the Son that was to suffer, but the Father, would, I believe, have straightway died[1] For "no one shall see God and live." If these things are so, it is certain that He who was seen at the end, was always seen from the beginning, and that He was not seen at the end who was not seen from the beginning, and that thus the seen and the unseen are two. Therefore the Son was always seen and the Son always moved about and the Son always "worked," by the authority and will of the Father, because "the Son can do nothing of Himself, unless He see the Father doing it," that is, of course, doing it in thought. For the Father acts by thought, the Son, who is in the Father's thought, sees and accomplishes.[2] Thus "all things were done by" the Son "and without Him nothing was done."[3]

<small>1 Tim 1. 17
1 Cor xv 3
1 Cor xv. 8
cf 1 Tim. vi 16
cf 1 Cor. xv 5-7,
John xxi. 2, etc.
cf Mark ix 6
Exod xxxiii 20
cf John v. 17
John v 19
John 1 3</small>

---

[1] Reading *amentiae* for *et amentia* with C H Turner For *ibidem* (like *ilico*) of time, cf Hoppe, p 112

[2] C H Turner compares Ignatius, *Epistle to the Ephesians*, § 3, but I am inclined to suggest *sinu* for the second *sensu* (cf John 1 18)

[3] On this punctuation of John 1. 3, see note on c 2

16 And you are not[1] to suppose that it was only the works[2] of the universe that "were done by the" Son; He also performed all that were subsequently performed by God. For "the Father" who "loves the Son and hath given over all things into His bosom,"[3] "loves," of course, from the beginning and "gave over" from the beginning, from that beginning[4] when "the Word was with God and the Word was God." To whom "has been given all power" by the Father "in heaven and on earth"; "the Father does not judge any one, but He has given all judgment to the Son," from the beginning, however. For in saying "all power" and "all judgment" and that "all things were made by Him" and that "all things have been handed over into His hand," he allows no exception in time, because it will not be a case of "all," if they have not belonged to all time. Therefore it is the Son who has judged from the beginning also, dashing to the ground the disdainful tower and destroying the tongues, punishing the whole world with violent waters, "raining fire and brimstone upon Sodom and Gomorrah," being God from God. It was He himself, too, who always condescended to converse with men, from Adam

cf. John i 3
John iii. 35
John i. 1
Matt xxviii. 18
John v 22
Matt xxviii 18
John v 22
John i 3
John iii 35
cf Gen xi 7, 8
cf Gen vii 10
cf Gen. xix 24

---

[1] For *nec* in a prohibitive clause, see Hoppe, p 107
[2] The works of the original creation (Gen 1)
[3] I follow the MSS here, with Oehler and the Colbertine MS (*c*) of the Gospels For abl. = acc , see Hoppe, pp 40 f Pamelius altered *sinu* to *manu*, and this is accepted by Kroymann *Sensu* in the apparatus to Kroymann's smaller edition is a misprint See c. 21 for the regular reading Ronsch, *Das N T. Tertullians* has strangely overlooked this difference
[4] Omit the *a* of MSS. with C. H Turner

down to the patriarchs and prophets, "in vision," cf Numb.
"in dream," "in a mirror," "in a riddle," building xii 6, 1 Cor. xiii
always from the beginning His course which He 12, Numb
was to maintain at the end. Thus it was that xii 8
even "God" was always learning the lesson "to cf Bar iii.
live on the earth with men," being none other than 36, 38
"the Word," which was to "become flesh", more- cf John i 14
over He was learning to pave[1] the way of faith
for us, that we might more easily believe that the
Son of God had descended into the world and
learn that something of the kind had been achieved
in the past. For it was "for us" that they were 1 Cor x
also done even as "they were written", "unto us 11
have the ends of the ages run down their course."
Even then He had actually such knowledge of
human feelings, as He was about to take upon
himself even the very materials of man, flesh and
mind,[2] when He asked Adam as if ignorant:
"Where art thou, Adam?" "regretting that He Gen iii 9,
had made man," as if not foreseeing his character, cf. Gen vi 6
"trying Abraham," as if He did not "know what cf Gen xxii 1
was in man"; when hurt, reconciled to them again, cf John ii 25
and any such qualities as heretics snatch at, as if
they were unworthy of God, for the dethronement
of the Creator, not knowing that these were suited
to the Son, who was to endure even the sufferings cf John
of men, thirst, hunger, tears, birth itself and death iv 7, xix 28, Matt
itself, having on this account been "made" by the iv 2, John xi 35; Matt i. 16; xxvii. 50, etc

---

[1] For the metaphorical uses of *sterno* in Tertullian, see Hoppe, p. 191.

[2] For parallels to this in Tertullian, see d'Alès, p 102

Father[1] "a little less than the angels" But you thrust upon the Father Himself what the heretics indeed will not consider suitable even to the Son of God, namely, the degradation of Himself by Himself for our sakes, although the Scripture says that one "was made less" by another, not Himself by Himself. And if it was One who "was crowned with glory and honour," it was Another who crowned Him—that is, the Father the Son And yet what an idea it is, that the all-powerful God, the invisible, "whom no man hath seen nor can see," He who "dwelleth in light unapproachable," He who "dwelleth not in what is made by the hand[2] of man," "in whose presence the earth trembles, the mountains melt like wax," "who seizes the whole world with his hand like a nest," whose "throne is heaven and his footstool earth," in whom is all space while He himself is not in space, who is the farthest boundary of the universe, the Most High, "walked in the garden till the evening" seeking Adam, and "shut the ark" after Noah's entrance, and "rested"[3] with Abraham "under an oak," and "called Moses from the" burning "bush," and appeared with three others "in the furnace" of the Babylonian king! Although He was called Son of God in "image" and "mirror" and "riddle,"

cf Ps viii 6 (Heb ii 7)
Ibid.
Ibid.
1 Tim vi 16
Acts xvii. 24
Ps xcvi 4, 5
Isa x 14
Isa. lxvi 1
cf. Gen iii 8
cf Gen. vii 16
cf Gen. xviii 4, 8
cf. Exod. iii 4
cf Dan iii 92
cf Numb xii 6, 8,
1 Cor xiii. 12.

---

[1] When Tertullian refers to this verse, it is rather the abased condition than the human nature of Christ he is thinking of: cf d'Alès, p 101 (p 100 n 3)

[2] For plur neut of participle following a preposition, see Hoppe, pp 97 f.

[3] For *refrigerare* intransitively used, see Hoppe, p. 64

these things, besides, would really not have been believed even about the Son of God, if they had not been in Scripture, and are perhaps not to be believed about the Father,[1] even though they are in Scripture; whom those people bring down into Mary's "womb" and "set upon" Pilate's "tribunal"[2] cf Matt and bury in "Joseph's tomb." This, then, makes 23 John xix. clear their mistake. Not knowing that from the 13 beginning the whole course of the divine system cf. Matt. xxvii 59, took its way through the Son, they believe that 60 the Father Himself was seen, met with men, worked, and endured thirst and hunger—in contradiction of the prophet's statement "The eternal Isa xl. 28 God will not thirst nor hunger at all" how much more will He neither die nor be buried!—and that thus one God, namely the Father, had always done what was done through the Son.[3] 17. They deemed it easier for the Father to come in the Son's name than for the Son to come in the Father's, although the Lord Himself says "I came in my Father's John v 43 name," likewise to the Father Himself "I have John xvii. made Thy name manifest unto men," while Scrip- 6 ture says in agreement·[4] "Blessed is He that Ps cxvii. cometh in the name of the Lord," meaning, of 26 course, the Son in the Father's name "But the Rev xix name of the Father," they say, is "God all- 6

[1] Here Tertullian is only giving a paradoxical turn to his argument

[2] From this reference it is obvious that Tertullian, or the version of Scripture used by him, took ἐκάθισεν transitively here, with Pilate as subject So also did the author of the Gospel of Peter (Turner)

[3] For this ending, see the note at the end of c 8

[4] For this use of *condico* in Tertullian, see Hoppe, p 127.

powerful," "Lord of hosts," "King of Israel," "I am" Because[1] so the Scriptures teach, we say that these also suited the Son, and that in these the Son came, and that in these He always acted, and that in this way He[2] made Himself clear unto men. "All things belonging to the Father," he says, "are mine."[3] Why not also names? When therefore, you read of "God all-powerful" and "the Most High" and "God of Hosts" and "King of Israel" and "I am," consider whether the Son also be not indicated by these terms, being in his own right "God," as "the Word of all powerful God" and as having "received power over everything", "Most High," as "raised by God's right hand," even as Peter says in his speech in Acts; "Lord of Hosts," because "everything has been made subject to Him" by the Father, "King of Israel," because the lot of that race fell[4] especially to him; also "I am," because many "are named sons, and are" not sons But if they will have it that the Father's name belongs also to Christ, they will get their answer in its proper place. Meantime let me have at this point an answer ready to that which they produce also from John's Apocalypse: "I am the Lord who is, and who

---

[1] *Quatenus* = "because"; see Hoppe, pp. 82 f.

[2] Reading *eum* for *ea in*, with C. H Turner

[3] Cf with d'Alès, p 100, cc 2, 22, for the equality of honour between the three Divine Persons.

[4] For various meanings and constructions of *excido* in Tertullian, see Hoppe, p. 131. He regards the meaning here as doubtful; possibly = *accidit*, which Fr Iunius read here, while Latini suggested *exiuit* Yet the MS reading is genuine; see passages from Livy in the lexica s v *excido*

was, and who comes with all power," and any other passages where they think that the title 'all-powerful God" is not suited also to the Son, as if He who is to come is not "all-powerful," although the Son of the "all-powerful" is also as "all-powerful" as God the Son of God [1]

18. But to prevent them from easily understanding this partnership in the Father's names which the Son enjoys, there is the confusion Scripture causes them, whensoever it lays down that there is one God only, as if it has not also set forth two Gods and Lords, as we showed above cf. c 13 "Therefore," they say, "because we find two and one, therefore both are one and the same, both Son and Father." But[2] Scripture is not in such danger that you need come to its help with your reasoning, lest it should seem inconsistent with itself. It is quite right both when it lays down that there is one God and when it shows that there are two, Father and Son, and it is self-sufficient. It is well known that the Son is named by it. For without prejudice to the Son it can quite rightly have defined God as one, whose the Son is. In having a Son He does not Himself cease to be One, in His own name, of course, as often as He is named apart from His Son. And He is named without the Son when He is defined in His supreme aspect as the chief being, which had to be put forward before the Son's name, because the Father

---

[1] For the ending, see the note on c 8.
[2] For *porro = sed*, etc., see Hoppe, p. 113

becomes first known, and after the Father the Son.
"One God" the Father, therefore, is named, "and other apart from" Him "there is none." When He Himself states this, He is not denying the Son, but any other god. Further, the Son is not other than the Father.[1] For examine what follows such announcements, and you will find that their teaching is generally connected with makers and worshippers of images, that the unity of divinity may drive out the multitude of false gods, a unity which nevertheless comprises the Son, who is as much to be reckoned in the Father as He is undivided and unseparated from the Father, though He is not named. Nay, if He had named Him, He would have separated Him, in these words: "There is none other but Me except My Son." For He would have made even the Son other, whom He would have excepted from the others. Suppose that the sun says. "I am the sun, and other than me there is not, except my beam"; would you not have stigmatised its folly, as if the beam also were not reckoned in the sun? Therefore it is that He said there was no other God but Himself. This word was uttered on account of the idolatry of the heathen as much as of Israel, also on account of the heretics who, even as the heathen fashion images with their hands, so also themselves fashion them with words, namely another God and another Christ. Therefore, even when He proclaimed Himself as one, the Father was acting in

[1] For *alius a*, see the notes on cc 8, 9 above.

the Son's interests, lest Christ should be believed
to have come from another God, rather than from
Him who had before said "I am God and other Isa xlv 5
than I there is none," who signified that He was
one, but in company with the Son, with whom
"He alone stretched out the heavens." cf Isa
19 If any will snatch even at this saying of His xliv 24
to prove His individuality, He uses the words, "I Isa xliv
alone stretched out the heavens" as meaning 24
"alone" in regard to all other powers, building
beforehand against the conjectures of heretics[1] who
maintain that the universe was constructed by
various angels and powers, who also either make
the Creator Himself into an angel or represent
Him as having been engaged by some other ex-
ternal power, even without His knowledge, to produce the works of the universe. Or, if He "alone cf Isa
stretched out the heavens" in the way in which xliv 24
these heretics perversely imagine, as an individual,
that "wisdom" would not be admitted, saying: Prov. viii
"When He was preparing the heavens, I was with $\substack{1 \\ \text{Prov viii}}$
Him" Isaiah[2] also said. "Who hath learned the 27
Lord's mind and who advised Him," except, of Isa xl 13
course, "Wisdom," which "was present" with Him cf. Prov.
and yet was within Him and "with Him con- $\substack{\text{viii. 1, 27} \\ \text{cf Prov.}}$
structed" all things, though He did not know what viii. 30
He was doing? "Apart from the wisdom," how-
ever, means "apart from the Son," who is "Christ, 1 Cor. 1
24

[1] The heretics intended are such as Simon Magus, Apelles, Menander, and others cf d'Alès, pp 110, 155, who refers to o her passages also where they are attacked
[1] *Esaias* Engelbrecht, *si* MSS

the wisdom and power of God" according to the Apostle, "who" alone "knows" the Father's mind. For "who knows what is in God save the Spirit that is in Him"? not that which is outside Him. There was therefore one who made God by Himself, only in the sense of apart from all others (but the Son). But let the Gospel also be rejected because it says that "all things were made by God through the Word and that without Him nothing was made."[1] Unless I am mistaken, it is also elsewhere written: "By His Word the heavens were strengthened and by His Spirit comes all their strength." But "the Word," "power and wisdom of God" will be the Son Himself. If, then, all things are through the Son, in "stretching out the heavens" also through the Son He did not "stretch them out alone," except in the way in which He did it apart from all others (but the Son). And, besides, He immediately speaks about the Son · "Who else cast down the signs of the ventriloquists and divinations from the mind, turning back the wise and making their counsel of none effect,[2] establishing the words of His Son"? saying, of course: "This is my beloved Son, hear Him." By thus adding "the Son" He Himself explains the manner in which "He alone stretched out the heavens," namely, alone with His Son, even as He is one with the Son. Similarly, also, the Son

---

[1] On this punctuation, cf the note on c. 2.
[2] This passage is closely parallel to Adv. Marc. iv. 22 (p. 217, Oehler, p. 494, l. 21, Kroymann)

will utter the words. "I alone stretched out the heavens," because "by the Word the heavens were strengthened," because when "wisdom stood by" in the Word, "the heavens were prepared" and "all things were done by the Word." It is fitting, also, that the Son "by Himself should have stretched out the heavens," since it was He alone who acted as servant to the operation of the Father. He also it will be that says. "I am the first, and I am for the time that is to come." "The Word," of course, is "first" of all: "In the beginning was the Word," in which beginning He was brought forth by the Father. But the Father as "having no beginning," as brought forth by no one, as unborn, cannot be seen. He who was always "alone," could have no order in time. *Isa. xliv. 24; Ps xxxii 6 cf Prov. viii. 27 John 1 3 Isa xliv. 24 cf Prov. viii. 27 Isa xli 4 cf Isa. xli. 4 John 1. 1 cf Heb. vii. 3 Isa xliv. 24*

Therefore if they thought that the same being was to be believed to be both Father and Son, with the object of asserting God to be one, His unity is unimpaired who, though He is one, has also a Son, who is Himself also in like manner included in the same Scriptures. If they refuse to consider the Son as second to the Father, lest "second" should bring about the mention of two gods, we have shown two Gods mentioned in Scripture also, and *c. 13* two Lords; and yet, lest this prove a stumbling-block to them, we explain why we should not speak of two Gods or Lords, but of two who stand in relation of Father and Son, and this not as the result of separation of being, but of arrangement, since we declare the Son to be undivided and unseparated from the Father, and different not in permanent condition, but only in rank, who although He is called God, when He is named by Himself, does not therefore imply two gods, but only one, by this very fact that He can be called God also from the unity of the Father.

20. But we must devote ourselves to the further repression of their reasonings,[1] if they pick anything out from the Scriptures to support their view, refusing to look upon everything else which in itself keeps the rule,[2] and indeed without danger to the unity of divinity and the established position[3] of monarchy   For as in the Old Testament they remember nothing but "I am God and other than I there is none," so in the Gospel they defend the Lord's answer to Philip   "I and the Father are one," and : " He who hath seen me, hath seen also the Father," and   "I am in the Father and the Father in me."   To these three passages[4] they would have the whole charter[5] of both Testaments to yield, although it is proper that the fewer passages should be understood in the light of the more numerous.   But this is a characteristic of all heretics.   Since there are few that can be found in

Isa. xlv. 5

John x 30, xiv 9

John. xiv 10, 11

---

[1] For examples of the dative of the gerundive and gerund in Tertullian, see Hoppe, pp 55 f

[2] *regulam seruant* "keeps the rule," that is, upholds the general teaching of Scripture   Probably there is no reference here to the *regula fidei*

[3] Reading *statu* with Kroymann for the not impossible MSS reading *sonitu* (*sonatu*), "meaning"

[4] Cf d'Alès, p 243

[5] One of the various expressions used by Tertullian to indicate Scripture   cf d'Alès, p. 224, Harnack, *Beitrage*, Bd. vi. (1914), pp. 137 ff.

20, 21] TERTULLIAN AGAINST PRAXEAS 81

the forest[1] of instances, these few they defend against the majority, and they take up the cause of the later against the earlier. But the rule that has been fixed for everything from the beginning, if valid in the earlier cases, gives directions also for the later, and of course also for the fewer[2]

21. Look therefore how many passages[3] lay down a rule for you even in the Gospel before Philip's consultation and earlier than any reasoning of yours And in the first place the very preface of the evangelist John at once points out what He who was to "become flesh," was in the past "In the beginning was the Word, and the Word was with God and the Word was God; He was in the beginning with God, all things were made by Him and without Him nothing was made."[4] For if these words may not be taken otherwise than as they are written, beyond doubt one is indicated who "was from the beginning," another "with whom" He was, the one "the Word" of God, the other "God"—although "the Word is" also "God," but as God's Son, not as Father—one "through whom" are all things, the other "from whom" are

cf John 1.
14
John 1 1-3

cf. John 1.
Ibid.

cf. Jol n 1.

---

[1] "forest" (*silua*), a graphic way of describing the immense size and complexity of Scripture cf *Apol* c. 4 (p 16, l 27, ed Mayor), *totam illam ueterem et squalentem siluam legum*, etc , of the mass of the ancient Roman jurisprudence It might be rendered "multitude" simply For this type of metaphor, see Hoppe, pp 194 f, especially p 195 n. 1

[2] The text is doubtful here, I translate Ursinus' *pauciora* (MSS. *paucioribus*)

[3] *quanta* here, as often in late Latin, = *quot* (sc *capitula*) cf. Hoppe, p 106

[4] For this punctuation of the verse, see the note on c 2

F

all things. But in what sense we use the word "other," we have already often announced, by "other" we must mean not the same—but not as if we meant separated by arrangement "other," not by division. He, therefore, it was that "was made Flesh," not He whose "Word" he was; it was *his* "glory that appeared, as of the only one from the Father," not as of the Father. "He" alone "explained the Father's bosom," the Father did not explain His own bosom. For the statement precedes: "God no one ever saw at any time." He also it is that is termed by John "the Lamb of God," not He whose "Beloved"[1] He is, who is certainly always called "Son of God," but not identified with Him whose Son he is. Nathanael perceived at once that He was this, even as elsewhere also Peter: "Thou art the Son of God." He himself, too, proves that they were right in this judgment, by answering Nathanael indeed thus · "Because I said, 'I saw thee under the fig-tree,' therefore thou believest," by maintaining, however, that Peter "was happy, since neither flesh nor blood had revealed" what he had thought, "but the Father who is in heaven." By this saying he established the distinction between the two persons . that of the Son on the earth whom Peter had recognised as "Son of God," and that of "the Father in heaven" who had "revealed" to Peter what Peter had

---

[1] *Dilectus* (Gk agapētos) see Dean Robinson, "*The Beloved*" *as a Messianic title*, in his Commentary on the Epistle to the Ephesians, pp 229-233

recognised, namely, that "Christ was the Son of God." When He entered "into the temple," He, as Son, called it His "Father's house." When He addresses Nicodemus, He says: "God so loved the world that He gave His only Son, that every one who believed in Him, should not perish, but should have everlasting life." And again · "For God sent not His Son into the world to judge the world, but that the world through Him might be saved; he who has believed in Him, is not judged, he who has not believed in Him, has been already judged, because he has not believed in the name of the only Son of God." John, too, when some one was asking about Jesus why "He baptized,"[1] said · "The Father loveth the Son and hath given all things into His hand; he that believeth in the Son, hath everlasting life, he that believeth not in the Son of God, shall not see God, but God's anger shall abide upon him." As what, indeed, did He show himself to the Samaritan woman? If as "the Messiah, that is called Christ," He showed Himself of course as the Son, not the Father, who elsewhere also was called "Christ, Son of God," not the Father. Later He says to His disciples. "It is mine to do the will of Him that sent me, that I may complete His work." And to the Jews about the healing of the paralytic · "My Father worketh hitherto, and I work." The Son says

Matt xvi. 16
John ii 14, 16
John iii 16

John iii. 17-18

cf John iii 26
John iii 35, 36

John iv. 25, 26
Matt xvi 16, etc.
John iv. 34
John v 17

---

[1] *cum interrogaret qui de Iesu, cur tingeret*, Kroymann's skilful emendation of the MSS. reading, *cum interrogaretur quid de Iesu contingeret*.

John v. 18 "the Father" and "I." For "on this account were the Jews the more desirous to kill Him, not only because He sought to do away with the Sabbath, but because He called God His Father, thus making Himself equal to God." Then, therefore, He said to them · "The Son can do nothing of Himself, save He see the Father doing it : for the things that He doth, the Son also doeth. For the Father loveth the Son and hath pointed out to Him all that He himself doeth, and greater works than these shall He point out [1] to him, that ye may wonder. For as He raiseth the dead and maketh them alive, so also the Son maketh alive those whom He will. Nor indeed does the Father judge, but He hath given all judgment to the Son, that all may honour the Son even as they honour the Father. He that doth not honour the Son, doth not honour the Father, who sent the Son. Verily, verily I say unto you that he who heareth the word and believeth Him that sent me, hath everlasting life and shall not come into judgment, but hath passed from death into life. Verily I say unto you that the hour shall come in which the dead shall hear the voice of the Son of God, and when they have heard it, shall live. For even as the Father hath everlasting life of Himself, so also He hath given to the Son to have everlasting life in Himself, and hath given Him to do judgment in power, because He is the Son of man," by the flesh, of course, even as He is Son of God by His spirit.

John v. 19-27

[1] *demonstrabit* Kroymann, for MSS. *demonstrauit*.

He adds further. "But I have greater testimony than that of John, for the works that the Father hath given me to complete will themselves bear witness concerning me, that the Father sent me; and the Father that sent me, Himself bore testimony concerning me." Moreover, in adding: "Ye have never heard His voice, nor yet have ye seen His shape," He proves that in the past it was not the Father, but the Son that was seen and heard. For He says· "I came in my Father's name, and ye received me not." Thus the Son was always in the name of God and King and All-powerful Lord and Most High.[1] Further, when they asked "what they ought to do," He answered: "To believe in Him whom God hath sent." He declares that He "is also the bread which the Father offered from heaven", therefore that "everything which the Father gave Him, was coming to Him, and that He would not reject Him, because He had come down from heaven, not to do His own, but the Father's will", that it was, moreover, 'His Father's will that he who saw the Son and believed in Him, should attain life and resurrection"; that "no one," further, "could come to Him unless the Father drew him"; "that every one who had heard and learnt from the Father, came to Him, adding here also. "not as if any one has seen the Father," to show that it is the Father's word that makes men learned. But when "many are departing" from Him and He puts the question to His

John v. 36, 37

John v 37

John v 43

John vi 28, 29

John vi. 32, 35

cf John vi. 37, 38

cf John vi 40

cf. John vi 44

cf John vi. 45

John vi 46

cf John vi 66

---

[1] See above, c 17.

apostles "whether they also wish to depart," what "does Simon Peter answer"? "Whither are we to go? Thou hast the words of life, and we believe that thou art the Christ." Did they believe that He was the Father or the Father's Anointed?

22 Whose teaching does He mean that they "wondered at"? His, or the Father's? When they were equally in doubt among themselves as to whether[1] He Himself were "the Christ" (of course not the Father, but the Son), He said: "And me, ye know whence I am, and I have not come of myself, but He is true, who sent me, whom ye know not; I know Him, because I was with Him." He did not say: "Because I am He" and "I myself sent myself," but "He sent me." Also, when "the Pharisees had sent to attack Him". "Yet a little while," said He, "I am with you and I go to Him who sent me." And when He denies that "He is alone"—"But I," he says, "and He who sent me, the Father"—does He not indicate two, as much two as inseparable? Nay, this was His whole teaching, that the two are inseparable, since also in setting forth the law confirming "the evidence of two men," He adds: "I give testimony concerning myself, and the Father who sent me testifies concerning me." But if He were one, provided the Son and Father were the same, He would not use the defence furnished by that law which imposes faith on "the testimony," not of one, but

---

[1] For this *ne* interrogative in an indirect clause, cf. Hoppe, p 72, and Mayor on *Apol.* c. 3 (p. 12, l 25).

"of two." Also, when asked "where the Father was," in "answering that neither He nor the Father was known to them," He mentioned two unknowns, because, "if they knew Him, they would know the Father," not indeed implying that He Himself was Father and Son, but because through their indivisibility the one could neither be recognised nor unknown without the other, while quite another passage of Scripture explains that they had not learned what He had said about the Father—"He who sent me,"[1] He said, "is true, and what I have heard from Him, that I also speak to the world" —when, of course, they ought to have learnt that the Father's words are in the Son, from reading in Jeremiah. "And the Lord said unto me, 'Behold I have put my words in thy mouth,'" and in Isaiah "The Lord gives me the tongue of learning to apprehend when I ought to speak a word," even as He Himself also says "Then shall ye learn that I am and that I speak nothing of myself, but even as He taught me, so also I speak, because He also that sent me is with me," and this, too, is evidence of two inseparables[2] Likewise in his dispute with the Jews, upbraiding them because "they wanted to kill him," He said: 'I speak what I saw with my Father," and "Ye do that which ye saw with your father," and: "Now ye wish to slay a man who hath spoken to you the truth which He heard from God," and: "If God had

cf John viii 19
John viii 19
Ibid.

John viii 26

Jer i 9

Isa l. 4

John viii 28, 29

cf John viii 37
John viii 38
John viii 40
John viii. 42

---

[1] The quotation is given by the MSS after the end of the clause in line 8, but Kroymann has transposed it to its present position
[2] For the ellipsis of *adtinet* or *pertinet* here, see Hoppe, p 146,

been your Father, ye would have loved me: for I proceeded and came from God,"—and yet we do not separate Him, although He said He "proceeded," in the way that certain people seize the chance offered by this utterance, for He "proceeded from" the Father like a beam from the sun, a stream from its source, a shrub from its seed. "I have not an evil spirit, but I honour my Father," and. "Were I to glorify myself, my own glory is nothing there is He that glorifieth me, the Father, who you say is your God and ye know Him not; but I know Him, and if I were to say: 'I know Him not,' I shall be, like you, a liar; but I know Him and I keep His word." And when He adds: "Abraham saw my day and rejoiced," of course He indicates that the Son had been seen of Abraham in the past, not the Father. Also over the blind man He says that He "must do the Father's works," to whom after restoring his eyes He says. "Dost *thou* believe in the Son of God?" and when he asked "who *He* was," He pointing to Himself, of course pointed out the Son, who He had said should "be believed." Later He declares that He "is known to the Father and that the Father is known to Him," and that therefore is "He loved by the Father because He lays down His life," because "He had received this command from the Father." And having been asked by "the Jews" "whether[1] He was Himself the Christ"—of course of God, for even to the present day the Jews hope, not for the

---

[1] \it = *num* see Hoppe, p 73.

Father Himself, but for the Christ (*i e.* Anointed) of God, because it is never written that Christ the Father will come—" I speak," He says, "to you, and ye believe not ; the works which I do in the Father's name, they themselves give evidence concerning me." Evidence of what ? Assuredly that He is Himself the very one about whom they were asking—that is, the Christ of God. With regard to his " own sheep " also He says that " no one will seize them from his hand ". " for what the Father hath given me is greater than all," and " I and the Father are one." Here, then, fools, or rather the blind, wish now to take a stand, because they do not see, first, that " I and the Father " is an indication of two , second, that " we are," at the end, being expressed in the plural, cannot come from one person only , third, that the expression is "we are one thing," not "we are one person." For if He had said . " We are one person," He could have supported their view , for " one (person) " appears to be an indication of the singular number But as matters are, when He says that two of the masculine gender are one in the neuter,[1] which is not connected with individuality but with unity, likeness, connexion, love of the Father who loves the Son, and the obedience of the Son who obeys the Father's will, in saying · " I and the Father are one thing," He shows that they are two whom He makes equal and joins together.[2] He further

John x 25

cf John x 27
John x 28
John x 29, 30

John x 30

Ibid

---

[1] On this passage, see d'Alès, p 82.
[2] *Ibid* , p 100

adds that He "had shown also many works from the Father, not any of which deserved stoning," and lest they should suppose that they ought to stone Him for the reason that He had desired Himself to be understood "as God Himself"—that is, the Father, because He had said: "I and the Father are one thing," indicating God as Son of God, not as God Himself—He says: "If in the Scripture it is written · 'I said: "Ye are gods,"' and the Scripture cannot be done away with, do ye contend that He whom the Father made holy and sent into the world, is a speaker of abusive language, because He said. 'I am the Son of God'? If I do not the works of my Father, do not believe, but if I do them and ye will not believe me, pray believe on account of the works; and know that I am in the Father and the Father in me" Through the works, therefore, the Father will be in the Son, and the Son in the Father, and thus through the works we know that "the Father and Son are one thing." All this He continued to impress upon them to the end that there might be believed to be two, though in one power only, because otherwise the Son could not be believed, unless two were believed.

cf John x. 32
cf John x. 33
John x. 30
John x. 34-38
cf. John x 30

cf John xi. 27
cf Matt. xvi. 16
John i. 49
cf. John xi 41

23. After this, too, "Martha' in confessing "Him Son of God," was no more in error than Peter and Nathanael, although, even if she had been in error, she would immediately have learned the truth. For, lo! when with a view to raising her brother from the dead the Lord "looked up to

heaven and his Father," He said (the Son, of course): "I thank Thee that Thou dost ever hear John xi me; for the sake of these crowds standing around 41, 42 I spoke that they might believe that Thou didst send me" But also 'midst "confusion of soul" cf John He said: "And what shall I say? Father, save xii 27 / John xii me from this hour? Nay, for this purpose came 27, 28 I into this hour; but, Father, glorify Thy name," the name in which the Son came. "I," says He, "came in John v 43 my Father's name," therefore[1]—for, of course, the voice of Son to Father had been enough[2]—lo! the Father gives a superabundant answer from heaven, He witnesses fully to the Son. "This is my Matt xvii beloved Son, in whom I am well pleased, hear 5 Him," and so also in this word · "I have glorified John xii and will glorify again." How many persons do you 28 think there are, most perverse Praxeas, if not as many as there are voices? You have the Son on earth, you have the "Father in heaven." This is Matt vi not a separation, but a Divine arrangement. But 9, etc we know that God is even amidst the depths and cf Ps is present everywhere, but in force and power, and cxxxviii 8 the Son being inseparable is with Him everywhere. Yet in the economy itself the Father wished the Son to be possessed on earth, but Himself in heaven, to which place also the Son Himself cf John looking up both prayed and besought the Father, xi 41 to which place He taught us, too, to raise ourselves

---

[1] For *inde* in causal sense (= "therefore"), a use rare even in Tertullian, see Hoppe, pp 111 f, who does not consider what follows *inde* here to be in parenthesis

[2] "had been enough '. that is, to secure the Father's agreement.

and pray.[1] "Our Father who art in heaven." Since He is also everywhere, this was His own seat that the Father desired: "To Me a throne." "He made" His Son "a little less than the angels"[2] by letting Him down to earth, but He was to "crown Him with glory and honour" by taking Him back into heaven. This distinction He was already offering to Him, saying "I have both glorified and will glorify." The Son requests from the earth, the Father promises from heaven. Why do you make both the Father and the Son liars? If either the Father was speaking from heaven to the Son, although He Himself was the Son in the earth, or the Son was praying to the Father, although He Himself was "the Father in the heavens,"[3] what sort of situation is it[4] that the Son should likewise beg of Himself in begging of the Father, if the Son was the Father; or again, that the Father should Himself promise to Himself in promising to the Son, if the Father was the Son! As for our speaking of two, divided from one another, in the way you gabble, it were more endurable to proclaim two divided than one God that changes His form. Therefore it was to these that the Lord then proclaimed: "It is not on my account that this voice has come, but on your

Matt vi 9
Isa lxvi 1
Ps viii 6 (Heb ii 7)
Ibid
John xii 28
cf Matt vi 9
John xii 30

---

[1] Cf *De Orat* 2, d'Alès, p 302
[2] Cf the note on c. 16, also d'Alès, pp 101, 155. Man is here considered on the material side only
[3] Reading *pater apud caelos* with Kroymann, for the *filius apud caelos* of the MSS.
[4] For this phrase, *quale est ut* (where *ut* is consecutive) cf. Hoppe, p 68. it is common in late authors.

account," that these also may believe that both the Father and the Son are each present in His own name and person and place. But "Jesus" further [1] "proclaims, saying· 'He that believeth in me, believeth not in me, but believeth in Him who sent me'"—because it is through the Son that people believe in the Father, and the Father is the authority for believing in the Son—"and he who looks at me, looks at Him who sent me." How? "Since," of course, "of myself I did not speak, but He who sent me, the Father, Himself gave me commandment what to say and what to speak;"—for "the Lord gives me a tongue of learning to learn the proper season for speech"— "the things that I speak, even as the Father told me, so also do I speak." How these things were said, the evangelist and, of course, so "beloved a disciple" as John knew better than Praxeas, and therefore he himself out of his own understanding said: "But before the festival of the Passover Jesus, knowing that all things had been handed over to Him by the Father and that He had gone out from God and was on His way to God." But Praxeas will have it that the Father Himself "went out from" Himself and "went away to" Himself, with the result that "the devil put into the mind of Judas" the betrayal "not of the Son, but of the Father Himself, with good result neither for the devil nor for the heretic, because not even in the case of His good Son did the devil work

John xii. 44

John xii. 45

John xii. 49

Isa l. 4

John xii. 50

cf John xix 26, etc

John xiii. 1, 3

cf John xiii 3
John xiii. 2

[1] For *adhuc = insuper, praeterea*, see Hoppe, p 110.

betrayal. For it was the Son of God that was
betrayed, who was in the Son of Man, even as the
Scripture adds : " Now is the Son of Man glorified,
and God is glorified in Him." What God ? Certainly not the Father, but the Word of the Father,
who was in the Son of Man, that is in the flesh.
In the flesh both when already glorified—but in
power and word—and previously, Jesus said : "And
God will glorify Him in Himself," that is, the Father,
the Son whom He "having Him in Himself," though
He has been sent forth to earth, will later glorify
by resurrection, after the defeat of death.[1]

24. There were clearly some who even then did
not understand, since even Thomas was for some
time unbelieving. For he said · " Lord, we do not
know whither thou goest, and how can we know
the road ? And Jesus said : I am the road, the
reality and the life : no one cometh to the Father
except through me , if ye had come to know me,
ye would have come to know the Father also , but
from now ye know Him and have seen Him."
And now we have reached Philip who, uplifted
with the hope of seeing the Father and not understanding how he should see the Father he had
heard of, said " Show us the Father, and it is
enough for us." And the Lord " said : Philip,
have I been so long time with you, and yet have
ye not come to know me ? " And as for Him who,
He says, ought to have become known by them—
for this is the only point that ought to be con

[1] For this type of metrical ending, see note on c. 1.

sidered—was it as Father, or as Son? If as
Father, let Praxeas teach us that Christ who had
"for so long a time" lived with them, could ever John xiv.
have been, I do not say understood, but even 9
considered as Father. For us all the Scriptures,
both Old and New, define the Christ (Anointed)
of God as the Son of God. This was preached
also in the past, this was proclaimed also by Christ
Himself, nay already even by the Father Himself,
who, before His face, avowed His Son "from the Matt. iii
heavens" and glorified His Son, "This is my Son," 17, etc
and "I have glorified and will glorify", this was John xii. 28
also believed by the disciples, this was also dis-
believed by the Jews Desiring them to hold this
belief about Himself,[1] every hour He named the
Father and set forth the Father and honoured
the Father. If that is so, therefore it was not the
Father who had lived with them "so long a time" John xiv
and whom "they had not known," but the Son, 9
and the Lord, when upbraiding them for not
recognising Himself to be Him of whom they had
been ignorant, wished, of course, to be recognised as
one whose non-recognition "for so long a time" He *Ibid*
had reproved, namely the Son. And it can now
be clear how it was that the words were uttered:
"He who seeth me, seeth the Father also," of *Ibid*
course in the same way as above: "I and the John x 30
Father are one";—why? Because "I went forth John xvi.
and came from God"—and· "I am the road, no 27, 28
one cometh to the Father but by me"; and: "No John xiv 6

[1] For acc and infin after a verb of "willing," cf. Hoppe, p 50

one cometh to me unless the Father hath drawn him"; and. "The Father hath handed over all things to me"; and "Even as the Father maketh alive, so also the Son", and · "If ye have come to know me, ye have come to know the Father also." According to these words He had presented Himself as the Father's substitute, through whom the Father might be seen in works and heard in words and His character learned in a Son who carried out the deeds and words of the Father, because the Father is invisible, a fact which Philip had learned in the Scripture and ought also to have remembered. "No one shall see" God "and live." And therefore he is reprimanded for his desire to see the Father, as if He were visible, and he is informed that He becomes visible in the Son by deeds of power, not by the visible manifestation of His person. For if he wished the Father to be understood as identical with the Son, in saying: "He that seeth me, seeth the Father," how did He add "Dost thou not believe that I am in the Father and the Father in me"? For He ought to have added [1]: "Dost thou not believe that I am the Father"? Or to what purpose did He amplify the argument, if He did not make that clear which He had wished to be understood, namely that He was the Son? Further, in saying: "Dost thou not believe that I am in the Father and the Father in me?" He preferred to amplify the argument for

---

[1] For the perf. infin after *debuerat*, where we should expect the present, see Hoppe, pp 53 f

the reason lest, because He had said "He who hath seen me, hath also seen the Father," He might be deemed to be the Father, a thing He never wished to be deemed, since He always declared Himself to be the Son and ' to have come from the Father." For this reason also He made clear the unity of the two persons, lest the Father should be desired by Himself as visible and face to face, and in order that the Son might be regarded as representing the Father,[1] and nevertheless He explained this also, namely how the Father was in the Son and the Son in the Father· "The words," He says, "which I speak unto you, are not mine"—of course because they are the Father's—"but the Father abiding in me doeth the works." "The Father," therefore, "abiding in" the Son through "the works" of power and "the words" of teaching, is seen through those things through which "He abides," and through Him in whom "He abides," and the special quality of each of the two persons shows itself from this very fact; namely, His saying: "I am in the Father and the Father in me." And further He says. "Believe." "Believe" what? "That I am the Father"? I do not think that is in Scripture, but. "That I am in the Father and the Father in me; otherwise, believe even on account of the works," those works, of course, through which the Father was seen in the Son, not by sight, but by thought.[2]

John xiv. 9
John xvi 28
John xiv. 10
John xiv. 11 *Ibid.*
Ibid.

---

[1] Literally "as the presenter of the Father to us" (in a moral aspect, cf d'Alès, p 359)
[2] For this metrical ending, see the note on c I

25. After dealing with [1] Philip and the whole compass of this enquiry which continues till the end of the Gospel, in the same tenor of conversation, in which Father and Son are each distinguished in His special quality, He promises that "He will ask a Paraclete also from the Father," after He has ascended "to the Father," and that He will send Him, and indeed "another (Paraclete)." But we have already explained how it is He is "another." [2] Further He says: "He will take from mine," even as He Himself "took from" the Father's. Thus the link with the Father in the Son and of the Son in the Paraclete makes three cleaving together, each to his neighbour. "These three are one thing," not one person, as it is put · "I and the Father are one thing," in respect to unity of nature, not as regards the singular number. Run farther over the Gospel and you will find that He whom you believe to be the Father, is called the Father's "vine," [3] and "the Father" is called "the husbandman," as being He who you suppose was on the earth and was at the same time recognised by the Son "in the heavens, when looking up" there He commended His disciples to "the Father." But even if it is not in this Gospel that these revelations are made : "My God, why hast Thou forsaken me?" and : "Father, into Thy hands I commit my spirit," yet

---

[1] For this pregnant use of *post*, cf. Hoppe, p 141
[2] For parallel passages, see d'Alès, pp 81, 82, 96.
[3] *uuem* Kroyn ann for the MSS. *uice*, very neatly.

after the resurrection and the glory of overcoming death, when the need for any humility was cast off,[1] when now He could have shown Himself as Father to so faithful a woman, who ventured to touch Him out of love, not out of curiosity or unbelief like that of Thomas, He said: "Do not touch me, I have not yet ascended to my Father, but go to my brethren"—because in this, too, He showed Himself the Son; for He would have called them "sons," if He had been the Father— "and you will say[2] to them, I go up to my Father and your Father, and my God and your God." Father to Father, and God to God? or Son to Father, and Word to God? For what purpose does even the very conclusion[3] of the Gospel confirm these writings except "That ye may believe that Jesus Christ is the Son of God?" Therefore, whatever of these words you think can benefit you in your effort to prove the identity of Father and Son, you will be striving against the final verdict of the Gospel.[4] The words "were" not "written with the purpose that you should believe Jesus Christ to be" the Father, but that you should believe Him to be "the Son."[5]

John xx. 17

John xx 31

Ibid.

---

[1] *exposita = deposita* see Oehler's note on *De Orat* 15.
[2] For the future indicative, implying a command, see Hoppe, pp 65 f
[3] It is unsafe to conclude from this expression that Tertullian was unacquainted with the twenty-first chapter of St John's Gospel (d'Alès, p 230, n 7, and Ronsch, p 290)
[4] "final". that is, from which there is no appeal.
[5] For the metrical ending, see the note on c. 8.

26. On account of the speech of Philip alone and the Lord's answer to him we seem to have run through John's Gospel, lest so many clear pronouncements, both of an earlier and a later date, should be overturned by one utterance,[1] which is to be interpreted rather according to, than against, everything, even against its own meaning. But to insert passages from other Gospels at this stage,[2] which confirm belief in the Lord's origin, it is enough that He who was to be born of a virgin, was named by the announcing [3] angel himself "Son of God": "The Spirit of God will come upon thee, and the power of the Most High will overshadow thee: wherefore the holy thing that will be born from thee, shall be called the Son of God." They will want, of course, to argue here too, but "the truth will prevail."[4] "Of course," they say, "'the Son of God' is God, and 'the power of the Most High' is the Most High." Nor are they ashamed to foist on those [5] words what, if it were true, would have been written. For of whom was he to stand in awe that he could not openly

Luke i. 35
Ibid

1 Esdr. iv. 41 f. Luke i. 35

---

[1] Elsewhere, also, Tertullian says we must proceed from the known to the unknown: cf d'Alès, p. 242 f.

[2] Reading *nunc* with Kroymann for *non* of the MSS, but it is possible that *alia* means "other than the one I am going to cite," and that the *non* should be retained.

[3] *adnuntiali*. Kroymann's palmary emendation for *adnuntiari* of MSS

[4] Note that the original has the present *praeualet* Tertullian is curiously in agreement with the popular way of quoting the expression

[5] Reading *illis* with Kroymann, for *illos* (*illo*) of MSS; but I feel sure neither about the reading nor about the interpretation.

declare, "God will come upon thee, and the Most High will overshadow thee"? But[1] by saying "the Spirit of God," although the Spirit of God is God,[2] yet by not explicitly naming God, he wished a portion of the whole to be understood which was to pass into the Son's person. Here "the Spirit of God" will be the same "Word."[3] For just as when John says: "The Word was made Flesh," we understand "the Spirit" also in the mention of "the Word," so also here we recognise "the Word" also in the name of "the Spirit" For besides, spirit is the foundation of speech, and speech is the working of spirit, and the two are one. But John would declare[4] that one "was made flesh," the angel would say that the other would become flesh, if spirit is not also word, and word spirit. Therefore, even as the Word of God is not the very Person whose word it is, so also the Spirit, even if it be spoken of as God's,[5] is yet not the very person whose it is said to be. Nothing belonging to a person will be the very person whose it is. Clearly, when something is from a person himself, and is (thus) his, provided it comes from himself, something can be such in character

cf Luke 1. 35

John 1 14

John 1 14; cf Luke 1. 35

---

[1] Cf cc 9, 14, and d'Alès, p 101

[2] I venture to suggest that *deus est* has slipped out after *spiritus dei*

[3] Here Tertullian seems to identify Son and Spirit, cf d'Alès, pp. 96 ff, 194, 252, and contrast cc 4, 8, 25 Justin had previously expressed the view taken in this chapter

[4] For the future indicative used = potential subjunctive, cf Hoppe, pp 64 f

[5] Reading *dei* with Kroymann for MSS *deus*

as he himself also is from whom it comes and whose it is, and therefore "Spirit" is God and "Word" is God, because from God, but, nevertheless, not Himself from whom it comes.[1] But if a God belonging to God, so to speak, a self-existent thing, will not be God Himself, but only so far [2] God as it comes from the being of God Himself, which is also a self-existent thing, and as some portion of the whole, much more "the power of the Most High" will not be the "Most High" Himself, because it is not a self-existent thing either, because it is spirit, just as neither wisdom nor providence is. These things, too, are not substances, but accidental attributes of each substance, and power is an accident of spirit but will not be spirit itself. These things, therefore, whatsoever they are, "the Spirit of God" and "the Word" and "the power," having been brought together into the virgin, "what is born of her is Son of God." That He was this He Himself testifies right from boyhood in these Gospels also. "Do ye not know," He said, "that I must be in my Father's house?" Satan, also, in his trials of Him knows that He is this. "If Thou art the Son of God": this also the evil spirits afterwards admit · "We know who Thou art, Son of God." He also Himself worships the Father. When recognised by Peter as "God's Christ" (Anointed), He does

Luke i. 35

Ibid.

Luke ii. 49

Matt. iv. 3, 6, etc.

cf. Mark i. 24, etc.

cf. Matt. xvi. 16, 17

[1] Tertullian's view is in error here, cf c 28, etc and d'Alès, p. 84.
[2] *hactenus . . . qua* an excellent instance of the original force of *hactenus*, cf Hoppe, p 111, n 1

not deny it. "Exulting in spirit" before the Father, "He says I offer praise[1] to Thee, O Father, that Thou hast hidden these things from the wise"—here also He asserts that "the Father is known to no one save the Son." It is the Son of the Father who "will before the Father confess knowledge of those that confess Him, and will deny knowledge of those that deny Him"; who "introduces" the parable of "the Son," not the Father, who "is sent into the vineyard after some slaves have been sent, and is slain by wicked rustics," and defended by the Father; who "even Himself is ignorant of the last day and hour, which are known only to the Father", who "arranges the kingdom" for His disciples "in the way" He says "it has been arranged for Himself also by the Father"; who "has the power to ask legions of angels" to His help "from the Father," if he will; who "calls aloud that God has abandoned Him"; who "places His spirit in the Father's hands"; and who after His resurrection binds himself "to send to His disciples the Father's promise"; and who at the last gives them command "to baptise into the Father and the Son and the Holy Spirit," not into one only. For it is not once only, but thrice that we are, at the utterance of each of the names, baptised into each of the Persons.[2]

Luke x 21
Luke x 22, etc.
cf Matt. x 32, 33, etc
cf Matt. xxi. 33–41, etc
cf Mark xiii 32
cf Luke xxii 29
cf Matt xxvi 53. cf. Matt. xxvii 46, etc
cf. Luke xxiii 46
cf Luke xxiv. 49
cf. Matt. xxviii. 19

---

[1] Or "thanks." The meaning of ἐξομολογοῦμαι is a well-known crux. The translator's *Pocket Lexicon to the Greek New Testament* may be consulted

[2] For the metrical ending, see the note on c. 8.

27. But why should I delay over such evident facts, when I ought to attack the arguments by which they seek to obscure the evident? For, refuted [1] on all sides by the distinction between the Father and the Son, which we set forth without disturbing the union, as in the case of the sun and the ray, the source and the stream, by what is yet the undivided number of two and three, they attempt nevertheless to explain it otherwise in accordance with their own view, so as to distinguish both alike in one person, Father and Son, saying that the Son is flesh (that is, man, that is, Jesus), while the Father is Spirit (that is, God; that is, Christ). And those who contend that Father and Son are one and the same, presently begin to separate them rather than to unite them. For if Jesus is different from Christ, the Son will be different from the Father, because the Son is Jesus and the Father is Christ. A monarchy of this kind they, perchance, learned about in Valentinus.[2] But cf. c. 26 this objection [3] of theirs also, the making of Jesus and Christ into two,[4] has already been parried by our previous discussion, which was to the effect that "the Word of God" or "the Spirit of God" and "the power of the Most High" are names given to Him whom they make out to be the

---

[1] For *obduco* = "refute," "convict," see Oehler or Mayor on Tert *Apol* 46, etc

[2] Cf *Adv Valent*, cc 19 27 (Oehler).

[3] *iniectio* = Greek *eisbŏlē* in Tertullian, see Hoppe, p 121

[4] Kroymann's transference of *duos facere Iesum et Christum* from their position in the MSS after *didicerunt*, appears to be right

Father. For they are not He Himself[1] whose they are said to be, but they are from Himself and belong to Himself. However, they will be refuted in another way, also, in the present chapter. "Lo," they say, "it was proclaimed[2] by the angel" "Wherefore the holy thing that will be born, shall be called the Son of God." "What was born," therefore, was flesh; therefore "the Son of God" will be flesh Nay, rather, it was with reference to the Spirit of God that the statement was made. For certainly it was "from the Holy Spirit that the virgin conceived,"[3] and what she conceived, that she bore; that therefore was to be born which had been conceived, and was to be borne—that is, spirit, whose "name also will be Emmanuel, which is translated[4] · 'God with us.'" Flesh, moreover, is not God, that it should be said about it "The holy thing shall be called Son of God," but He who was born in it, is God, concerning whom also the psalm says[5] Since "man was born God in it, and built it by the Father's will." What "God was born in it"?[5] "The Word," and the Spirit who with "the Word was born of the Father's will." Therefore,[6] since

Luke 1 35

Creeds

cf Matt 1 23

Luke 1 35

Ps lxxxvi.

John 1 13

---

[1] *ipse* with Kroymann, *ipsae* MSS
[2] In such cases it is tempting to alter to *praedictum*, but see the index to Mayor's Tertullian *Apologeticus* (Cambr Press, 1917) s v. On the thought, cf c 26, and d'Alès, p 194
[3] On this passage see d'Alès, p 97, and cf c 26
[4] For *interpretari* passive, see Hoppe, p 62.
[5] This quotation (repeated below, p 107), is very free, and Tertullian's exegesis is unwarrantable
[6] Perhaps the most important Christological passage in Tertullian; see d'Alès, p. 198.

the Word is in the flesh,[1] we must enquire also into this, how "the Word became flesh," whether as having been changed to the form of flesh or as having put on flesh as a covering.[2] Certainly the latter. But it must be believed that God is unchangeable and incapable of outward form, as being everlasting. Moreover, change of form implies the destruction of the original form.[3] For everything that is altered in shape to become something else, ceases to be what it has been, and begins to be what it was not. God, however, neither ceases to be, nor can be anything else. But "the Word is God" and "the Word of the Lord abideth for ever," continuing, of course, in its own shape And if it is not possible that the Word should be changed in shape, it follows that He must be understood to "have been made flesh" in this sense, namely by being made in flesh and manifested "and seen and handled" by means of flesh, because other considerations also demand that it should be understood in this way. For if "the Word" by a change in the form and a change in substance "became flesh," Jesus will then be one substance composed of two, flesh and spirit, a sort of mixture, like electrum made from gold and silver, and it begins to be neither gold (that is,

---

[1] D'Alès, p 87, sets forth parallels between this passage and early Greek Fathers Here I translate Kroymann's order *dum sermo in carne* for the MSS order *sermo in carne dum*

[2] For *utrumne .. an*, cf Hoppe, p 73

[3] Cf. Lucretius, I 670–671, etc This passage has a bearing on the doctrine of transubstantiation, cf. d'Alès, p. 363, n. 1.

spirit) nor silver (that is, flesh), since one element is interchanged with the other, and a sort of third substance is the result. Therefore Jesus will neither be God—for "the Word" ceased to exist, "being made flesh"—nor man. He who was "Word" is not "flesh" in a real sense. So neither comes from both, and the third is far different from both. But in truth we find him definitely explained as both God and man, and this is suggested by the psalm itself: Since "man was born God in it, and built it by the Father's will"; certainly everywhere Son of God and Son of Man, as being both God and man, differing undoubtedly in His own special character according to both natures, because neither is "the Word" other than "God," nor the flesh other than man. So also the Apostle teaches about both his natures· "Who was made," he says, "of the seed of David"; He will be man and the Son of Man, "who was marked as Son of God according to the spirit". he will be God and the Word, the Son of God. We see two natures, not mixed, but joined together in one person, God and man, Jesus—I postpone speaking[1] of Christ—and so unimpaired is the special quality of both natures, that on the one hand spirit carried out its own operations in Him—that is, deeds of power and works and signs—and on the other hand flesh experienced its own sufferings, "starving" in the devil's company, thirsting in the company of

cf John 1. 14

Ps lxxxvi. 5

Rom 1. 3

Rom. 1. 4

cf Matt. iv. 1, 2, etc

cf John iv. 7

---

[1] For the ellipsis of the verb of saying, cf. Hoppe, p. 146.

"the Samaritan woman," "weeping" for Lazarus, "anxious even unto death," and finally died. But if there were some third thing, a mixture of both, like electrum, no such clear proofs of two natures would show themselves, but on the one hand the spirit would have acted carnally, and on the other the flesh would have acted spiritually as the result of the change, or neither carnally nor spiritually, but after some third pattern, as the result of the mixture. Nay, rather, either "the Word" would have died or "the flesh" would not have died, if "the Word" had been turned into "flesh"; for either "the flesh" would have been immortal or "the Word" mortal. But because both natures, each in its own established condition, acted separately, therefore both their works and their outcomes corresponded to them. Learn, therefore, with Nicodemus that "what is born in flesh is flesh, and what is from spirit is spirit." Neither does flesh become spirit nor does spirit become flesh. But they can, to be sure,[1] be present in one Of these Jesus consisted, as man, of flesh, as God, of spirit. In respect of that part which was spirit, the angel then declared Him "Son of God," keeping for the flesh the name "Son of Man." So also the Apostle by calling him "mediator between God and men," established his double nature. Lastly · you who explain "the Son of God" as flesh, show me who is "the Son of Man." Can He be the Spirit? But you wish

---

[1] For *plane* in this sense (often ironical), cf. Hoppe, p. 112

the Spirit to be regarded as the Father Himself, because "God is a spirit," as if there were not also a "Spirit of God," just as there is both a "God" who is "Word" and a "Word of God."[1]

John iv. 24, etc
Matt iii 16, etc

28. Therefore you make Christ the Father, you fool, who do not even examine the force of this name, if indeed "Christ" is a name, and not rather an appellative · for it means "anointed." "Anointed," moreover, is no more a name than "clothed," than "shod," something which is an accidental quality of a name. If as the result of some argument Jesus were to be called also "clothed," just as Christ gets his name from the mystery of anointing, would you call Jesus "Son of God" in the same way, but believe "clothed" to be the Father? Apply this now to Christ. If the Father is Christ, the Father was anointed, and of course by some one else, or if by Himself, prove it. But this is not the teaching of the Acts of the Apostles in that cry of the Church to God "For all, yea, Herod and Pilate with the nations, have assembled in this city against Thy holy Son,[2] whom Thou didst anoint. So they testified that Jesus was both "Son of God" and "Son anointed" by the Father. Therefore Jesus will also be Christ who was "anointed" by the Father, and not the Father

Acts iv 27

---

[1] For the metrical ending, see the note on c 1
[2] Kroymann is wrong in adding *Iesum* here Tertullian omits it also at *Bapt* 7 Besides MS. *gigas* of Acts quoted by Wordsworth and White, a quotation in the eighth-century Spanish compiler Beatus, *in Apocalypsin*, omits (ed. E. S Buchanan, *Sacred Latin Texts*, iv. London, 1916)

who "anointed the Son." So also Peter teaches:
Acts ii 36 "Let the whole house of Israel therefore learn with absolute certainty that God made Him, this Jesus, whom *ye* have crucified, both Lord and Christ"— that is, 'anointed.' John, moreover, even brands him
1 John ii. 22 as "a liar, who denies that Jesus is Christ," but, on
1 John v 1 the contrary, says "every one who believes that Jesus is the Christ, is born of God." For this
1 John iii 23 reason he also exhorts us "to believe in the name of His Son Jesus Christ," in order, of course,
1 John i. 3 that "we may have communion with the Father and His Son Jesus Christ." So also Paul every-
cf. 1 Cor i. 3, etc. where puts "God the Father and our Lord Jesus
Rom. 1. 8 Christ." When he writes to the Romans, he "gives thanks to God by our Lord [1] Jesus Christ"; when he writes to the Galatians, he declares he is
Gal. i. 1 "an apostle not from men nor through a man, but through Jesus Christ and God the Father." And you have his whole body of writings, which pro-
cf. 1 Cor. 1 3, etc. claim after this fashion and set forth two, "God the Father" and "our Lord Jesus Christ," Son of the Father, and that Jesus Himself is the Christ,
Luke 1. 35, etc. who is also, under another name, "Son of God." For it follows that, by the right by which both names belong to one, namely, to the Son of God, even one of the two without the other belongs to the same. And if on the one hand Jesus alone is mentioned, Christ also is understood, because Jesus was anointed, and if on the other

---

[1] "our Lord" seems to be absent from all other authorities for the text of this verse

hand Christ alone is mentioned, He is the same
as Jesus, because Jesus was anointed. Of these
names the one is His own, which was conferred by cf Matt. i. 21
the angel, the other is an accidental attribute,
which comes from anointing, so long, however,
as Christ is Son, not Father. Finally: how blind
is he who does not understand that in the name
of Christ another God is set forth, if he attribute
the name of Christ to the Father! For if Christ
is God the Father who says: "I ascend to my John xx. 17
Father and your Father, and to my God and your
God," of course He points to another Father
and God above Himself. If, further, Christ is the
Father, it is some one else "who stablishes the Amos iv. 13
thunder and creates the wind and preaches His
Christ (Anointed) among men." And "if the Ps ii 2
kings of the earth have stood by and the rulers
have been assembled together against His own
Christ (Anointed)," it will be another Lord
"against whose Christ (Anointed) the kings and cf. Ps ii 2
rulers have been assembled." And if "the Lord Ps cix. 1
says this to my Lord Christ" (Anointed), it will
be another Lord who speaks to the Father of
Christ. And when the Apostle writes: "That Eph i. 17
the God of our Lord Jesus Christ may give you
a spirit of wisdom and knowledge," it will be
another God of Christ Jesus who giveth liberally
of spiritual endowments. Assuredly, not to wander Rom. viii. 11
away altogether, "He who raised Christ, and who
will raise our mortal bodies also," will be a sort cf. 1 Cor. xv. 3, 4
of different raiser from the Father "who died and Creeds

was raised," if so be that Christ who died, is the Father [1]

29. Silenced, I say silenced be this evil-speaking, enough that Christ, the Son of God, is spoken of as dead, and that too because it is so written. For the Apostle also, in declaring not without sorrow that "Christ died," added [2]: "according to the Scriptures," in order to soften the harshness of the declaration by the authority of the Scriptures and to destroy an obstacle in the hearer's path. And yet, since there are two natures present [3] in Christ Jesus, a divine and a human, and it is certain that the divine is immortal, while the human is mortal, it is clear how far he speaks of him as "dead," namely, so far as He was flesh and man and Son of Man, not in so far as He was "Spirit" and "Word" and "Son of God." Finally, in saying. "Christ died"—that is, the Anointed (died) [4]—he showed that what was anointed died—that is, the flesh. "Therefore," you say, "we, too, in speaking of the Son in the same way as you do, speak no evil against the Lord God; for it is not as regards his divine, but as regards his human nature that we speak of him as dead." But yet [5]

1 Cor xv. 3

---

[1] For the metrical ending, see the note on c 11.

[2] The better MSS read *adicit*, which may be right, in spite of the following *molliret* and *euerteret*. On such sequences see Hoppe, p. 67

[3] *Censeantur* on the meanings of this word in Tertullian see Thes s v or d'Alès, pp 366 f

[4] See d'Alès, p 363 n 3 (p 364), on this passage, and its bearing on the Eucharistic doctrine of Tertullian

[5] I translate Kroymann's *at tamen*, but I am by no means certain that it is right; the MSS. read *at cum*.

you speak evilly, not only because you say that the Father died, but also because you say He was crucified. For you are speaking against the Father when you turn the curse [1] of the crucified, which according to the Scripture belongs to the Son—because "Christ was made a curse for you," Gal. iii 13 not the Father—when you turn the curse, which is Christ, upon the Father. But we, when we speak of "Christ as crucified," do not speak evil of Him, 1 Cor. i. we are only recalling the curse in the law; for [23] the Apostle when he said this, did not speak evil either. Just as no evil-speaking is employed in speaking of one of whom something can be truly said, so it is evil speaking, if what is said cannot be said with truth. Therefore the Father did not suffer even in company with the Son. It is, of course, because they are afraid of explicit evil-speaking against the Father that they hope it will be lessened in this way—allowing now that Father and Son are two—if the Son indeed suffers, but the Father suffers with him. They show themselves fools in this as well. For what is fellow-suffering but [2] to suffer along with another? Again, if the Father cannot suffer, assuredly He cannot be a fellow-sufferer, or if He can be a fellow-sufferer, He can, of course, suffer. You confer nothing on Him even by your fear. You fear to speak of Him as able to suffer who, you

---

[1] Reading *maledictionem* with Kroymann for *maledictio* of the MSS.
[2] *quam = nisi* after a suppressed *alius* cf Hoppe, p 77

say, can be a fellow-sufferer. But the Father is just as incapable of being a fellow-sufferer as the Son also is incapable of suffering as regards that nature which makes him God.[1] But how did the Son suffer, if the Father did not also suffer with Him? He is separated from the Son, but not from the God. If a river,[2] too, is polluted by some disturbance, although one material only runs down from the source and is not separated from the source, yet the pollution[3] of the stream will have nothing to do with the source; and although it is the source's water that suffers in the stream, since it suffers, not[4] in the source, but in the stream, it is not the source that suffers, but the stream which comes from the source. So also the Spirit of God, although[5] it might suffer in the Son, because it would not suffer in the Father, but in the Son, would not seem to have suffered as the Father. But it is enough that the Spirit of God suffered nothing in its own name, because if it suffered anything in the Son, this[6] would really mean that the Father suffered with the Son in the flesh. This is a matter for reconsideration. Nor will any one deny it, since we also cannot suffer for God, unless the Spirit of God be in us, who also

---

[1] See d'Alès, pp 98 f. on this passage

[2] The parallel here is explained by Hoppe, p. 198

[3] *iniuria* is sometimes found in late authors in the passive sense of "damage," "harm" cf. Hoppe, pp 121 f.

[4] For *non = ne* in this phrase, cf Hoppe, p 79

[5] Keep *qui* of the MSS here, and take it concessively · see also d'Alès, p 97

[6] Supposing *hoc* omitted after *filio*. The text here is corrupt I have tried to make some sense out of the MSS reading

speaks concerning us what belongs to confession, not that He Himself suffers, but that He gives the power to suffer.

30. If in spite of what I have said you mean to proceed[1] farther, I shall be able to answer you more harshly and to put you in conflict with the declaration of the Lord Himself, so as to say: "Why do you enquire about this subject?" You have Himself "crying aloud" at the passion · "My God, my God, why hast Thou forsaken me?" Matt. xxvii 46 Therefore, either the Son was suffering, having been abandoned by the Father, and it was not the Father who suffered, who forsook the Son; or if it was the Father who was suffering, to what God did He cry aloud? But this speech of flesh and soul (that is, of man), not an utterance of Word or Spirit (that is, not of God) was uttered for the purpose of showing that God could not suffer, who thus forsook the Son in "handing over" his human nature "to death." Isa. liii 12 The Apostle also was of this opinion when he wrote: "If the Father spared not the Son"; Rom. viii. 32 this also Isaiah earlier proclaimed: "And the Lord handed Him over for our sins." Isa. liii. 6 He "forsook" Him in "not sparing" Him, He "forsook" Him in "handing Him over." cf Matt. xxvii 46 cf. Isa But the Son was not "forsaken" by "the Father in whose liii. 12 hands the Son placed His spirit." cf. Luke xxiii. 46 For He placed it there and immediately died; for if the spirit Ibid remains in the flesh, the flesh cannot die at all. So "to be forsaken" by the Father meant death cf Matt. xxvii. 46

---
[1] Reading *perges* with Kroymann, for *pergens* of the MSS.

for the Son. The Son therefore both "dies" and is "raised again" by the Father "according to the Scriptures," the Son "ascends to the topmost" regions of heaven, who "also descends into the lowest[1] parts of the earth." It is "He that sits at the Father's right hand," not the Father who sits at His own It was He whom Stephen saw, when he was being "stoned," still "standing at God's right hand," as one who would thereafter "sit, until the Father should put all His enemies under His feet" for Him. It is He also who is "to come" again on "the clouds" "of heaven in such wise as He also ascended." It was He that meantime gave forth the gift he had received from the Father, "the Holy Spirit," the third name of divinity and the third stage of majesty, the preacher of one monarchy, but also the expounder of economy, if any one receive the words of his new prophecy,[2] and "the leader into all truth," which is in the Father and Son and Holy Spirit according to the Christian mystery.[3]

cf. 1 Cor. xv. 3, 4
cf Eph. iv. 8, 9
cf. Mark xvi. 19
cf Acts ii 34
cf. Acts vii. 58, 55
cf. Ps. cix. 1
cf. Acts i 11
cf. Luke xxi. 27
cf. Acts ii. 4
John xvi. 13

31. But this attitude of yours belongs to the Jewish faith, I mean the belief in one God in such a way as to refuse to count the Son along with Him, and after the Son the Holy Spirit. For what will there be between us and them except this difference? What need is there of the Gospel,

---

[1] Reading *inferiora*, as the contrast with *superiora* requires, even apart from the undoubted allusion to Eph. iv. 9. The confusion of *interior, inferior* and *intra, infra* occurs elsewhere also in MSS.

[2] On this passage in Tertullian, see d'Alès, p. 450, n 2.

[3] For the metrical ending here, see the note on c. 1.

which is the foundation of the New Testament, laying it down that "the Law and the Prophets were until John,"[1] if the Father and Son and Holy Spirit, "three" objects of belief, do not thereafter establish one God? God wished to make the mystery new in such a manner that He should be believed to be One in a new way through the Son and the Spirit, that He should now come to be known as God face to face in His own special names and persons, who though preached in the past also through the Son and the Spirit, was not understood. "The antichrists," therefore, had better look out, "who deny Father and Son." For they deny the Father in saying that the Son is identical with Him,[2] and they deny the Son in believing that the Father is identical with him, offering them what they are not and taking away from them what they are. But "he who confesses[3] that Christ is the Son of God," not the Father, "God remains in him and he himself in God." We believe "God's testimony" in which He gave evidence concerning His Son. "He who hath not the Son, hath not life either." But he too "hath not the Son," who believes him other than the Son."[4]

Luke xvi. 16
cf. 1 John v. 8
1 John ii. 22
1 John iv 15
cf 1 John v. 10
1 John v. 12

---

[1] Tertullian refers to this verse elsewhere · see Ronsch, *das N T Tertullians*, ad loc , d'Alès, p 174, n 6.

[2] For *dum* with indic here = coincident *cum*, see Hoppe, p. 79

[3] The future perfect (or perfect subjunctive) here is an exact translation of the original Greek taken as Latin, such a use supports the contention that originally the fut perf expressed absolute (not relative) futurity It certainly occurs frequently where, according to our feeling, the ordinary future, or even the present, would suit the context · cf Hoppe, p 66

[4] For the metrical ending here, see the note on c 1.

INDEX OF QUOTATIONS AND REFERENCES

OLD TESTAMENT (SEPTUAGINT)

	PAGE		PAGE
Gen. 1 1	cf 35	Deut v 7	cf 60
1 3	39, 56	v 11 .	cf 44
1 6	. 56	xvii 6	. 86
1 7	56	xxxii 8	cf 74
1 14	56	xxxii 9	cf. 74
1. 16	. 56	1 Esdr iv 41	. 100
1 26	54, 55, cf 37, 38, 55	Ps ii 2	111, cf. 111
1 27	. . . 55	ii 7	. 40, 51, cf 51
ii 7	cf 37, 55	iii 2	. . . 53
iii 8	cf. 72	viii 6	. cf 46, 72 *ter*, 92 *bis*
iii 9	71	xxxii. 6	. 40, 41, 78, 79
iii 22	54, 55	xliv 2	40, 51, cf 51
vi 6	cf 71	xliv 7	. 57
vii 10	cf 70	xliv 8	57
vii 16	cf 72	lxx 18	53
xi. 7, 8	cf 70	lxxxi 1	59
xii 7	cf. 62, 64, 65	lxxxi 6	59
xviii 4	cf 72	lxxxvi 5	105, 107
xviii 8	. cf. 72	xcvi 4, 5	. . 72
xviii. 14	cf 49	cvi 20	. 37
xix 24	cf 58, 70	cix 1	34, 53, 58, 111, cf. 116
xxii 1 .	cf 71		
xxviii. 13	cf 62, 64, 65	cix 3	40, cf. 51
xxxii 30	63, 65, cf 62	cxvii. 26	. 73
Exod iii. 4	. cf. 72	cxxxviii 8	cf 91
iii 14	74 *bis*	Prov viii. 1	77, cf. 77
xx. 3 .	cf. 60	viii 22 .	38, 39, 40 *bis*, cf 51
xx 7	. 42	viii 23 .	. . 38
xxxiii 11	. 63	viii. 25 .	. 38, 40, cf 51
xxxiii. 13	. 62	viii 27 .	38, 39, 77, cf 77, 79
xxxiii. 20	. 62 *bis*, 69, 96, cf. 63, 65 *ter*, 66		
		viii 28	. 38
Numb. xii. 6–8	. . 64	viii 30	. . 38, cf. 77
xii. 6	. . cf. 71, 72	Job xlii. 2	. 49, cf 49 *ter*, 50
xii 8 .	64, 67, cf. 64, 65, 71, 72	Wisd. xi 23	. . cf 50
		Amos iv. 13	. 111
xxiv, 16	. . . 74	Isa 1. 9 .	. . 74 *bis*

INDEX OF QUOTATIONS

	PAGE
Isa vi. 1	cf. 62
x 14	72
xl 8	106
xl 13	77
xl 28	73
xli. 4	79, cf. 79
xlii 1	. 52
xliv. 6	74 *bis*
xliv 24	77, 79 *ter*, cf 77 *bis*, 78 *ter*
xliv. 25, 26 .	78
xlv. 1 .	. . 53
xlv 5 .	76, 77, 80, cf 76
xlv 14.	. . . 57
xlv. 15 .	57
Isa. xlix 6	. 53
l 4 .	87, 93
liii. 1, 2	. 53
liii. 1	58
liii 6	115
liii. 12 .	115, cf. 115
liv. 1	cf. 49
lxi 1	cf 53
lxvi 1 .	72, 92
Jer. i 9 .	. 87
Bar iii 36, 38	cf. 71
Lam. iv. 20	. 66
Ezek. i. 1	cf. 62
Dan. iii. 92	cf 72
vii. 10	32

NEW TESTAMENT

	PAGE
Matt 1. 16	. cf 28, 71
i 21	. cf 111
i 23	cf 49, 73, 105
iii. 12	. cf. 28
iii 16	. . 109
iii 17	. 95, cf. 82
iv. 1, 2	cf 107
iv 2	. cf. 71
iv 3	. . 25, 102
iv. 6	25, 102
v 14	. cf 61
v. 16	. cf. 61
v 37	47
vi. 9 .	. 91, 92, cf. 92
viii 20	108
x 32	. cf 103
x. 33	. cf 103
xi 27	cf 43, 74, 96
xiii 7	. cf 28
xiii 25	cf 27
xiii 30	cf 28
xiii 41	cf 28
xvi. 16	82 *bis*, 83 *bis*, cf 90, 102
xvi 17	82 *bis*, cf. 102
xvii 1	. cf 64
xvii. 3	. cf. 64
xvii. 5	. . . 91
Matt xxi 33–41	. cf 103
xxvi 38	. cf 108
xxvi 53 .	cf. 32, 103
xxvii 46 .	98, 115, cf. 103, 115 *bis*
xxvii 50 .	. cf 71, 108
xxvii 59, 60	. cf. 73
xxviii 18 .	70 *bis* cf. 74
xxviii 19	cf 103
Mark 1 24	cf 102
ix 4	cf. 64
ix 6	cf. 69
xiii. 32	cf 103
xvi. 19	cf. 116
Luke i 35 .	100 *bis*, 102 *bis*, 105 *bis*, 108, 110, cf. 100, cf. 101 *bis*
ii 49	102
iii 22 . .	40, 51, cf. 51
iv. 9–11	cf. 25
iv 18	. 53
ix. 30	cf. 64
ix 35	78
x 21	103
x 22	. 103
xvi 16	. 117
xviii. 27	. 49
xxi. 27 .	. cf. 116

INDEX OF QUOTATIONS

Luke xxii. 29	cf. 103
xxiii 46	98, cf. 103, 115 *bis*
xxiv 49	cf 103
John i. 1–3	78, 81
i. 1	36, 42, 44, 56, 58, 67 *bis*, 68, 70, 79, 106, cf 68, 81, 108
i. 2	26, 67
i. 3	28, 40, 41, 56, 69, 78, cf 70, 81
i. 4	cf. 56
i 9	56
i. 12	cf 59
i. 13	105
i. 14	67 *bis*, 68 *bis*, 82 *bis*, 101 *bis*, 106 *bis*, cf 40, 71, 81, 106, 107, 108
i 18	43, 66 *bis*, 67, 68 *bis*, 82 *bis*, cf. 62
i. 36	82, cf. 82
i. 49	82, cf 91
i 50	82
ii. 14	83
ii. 16	83
ii 25	cf. 71
iii. 6	108
iii 16	83
iii 17, 18	83
iii 26	cf. 83
iii 35, 36	83
iii 35	70 *bis*
iv 7	cf. 71, 107
iv 24	42, 109
iv. 25, 26	83
iv 34	83
v 17	83, cf. 69
v. 18	84
v. 19–27	84
v. 19	69, cf. 43
v. 21	96
v. 22	70
v. 28	86
v. 36	85
v. 37	85 *bis*
v 43	73, 85, 91
vi. 28, 29	85
vi. 32	85
John vi. 37, 38	cf. 85
vi 38	cf. 34, 44
vi. 40	cf. 85
vi. 44	96, cf 85
vi. 45	cf. 85
vi 46	85
vi 66	cf. 85
vi 67	cf. 86
vi 68, 69	86
vii 26, 27	cf 86
vii 28, 29	86
vii 32, 33	86
viii 12	61
viii 16	86, cf. 86
viii 17	86 *bis*
viii 18	86, cf. 86
viii 19	87, cf 87
viii 26	87, cf. 44
viii 28, 29	87
viii 37	cf 87
viii 38	87
viii 40	87
viii 42	87, 88 *bis*
viii 44	cf 26
viii 49	88
viii. 54, 55	88
viii 56	88
ix 4	cf. 88
ix 7	cf 88
ix 35	88, cf. 88
ix 36, 37	cf. 88
x. 15	cf 88
x 17	cf 88
x 18	cf. 88
x 24	cf. 88
x 25	89
x 27	cf. 89
x 28	89
x 29	89
x. 30	41, 80, 89 *ter*, 90, 95, 98, cf 90
x 32	cf. 90
x 33	cf. 59, 90
x. 34–38	90
x 34	cf. 59
xi. 27	cf. 90
xi 35	cf. 71, 108
xi. 41	91, cf. 90, 91

INDEX OF QUOTATIONS

Reference	Page	Reference	Page
John xi. 42	91	Acts ii. 4	cf. 116
xii. 27	91, cf. 91	ii. 33	cf. 74
xii. 28	91 *quater*	ii. 34	cf 116
xii. 30	92	ii. 36	110
xii. 36	60	iv 27	109
xii. 44	93	vii. 55	cf 116
xii. 45	93	vii 58	cf 116
xii. 49	93, cf. 44	xv. 19	cf. 60
xii 50	93	xvii 24	72
xiii 1	93	Rom. i. 3	107
xiii. 2	93	i. 4	107
xiii 3	93, cf 74, 93	i 7	61
xiii 31	94	i 8	110
xiii 32	94	i. 20 (?)	cf. 42
xiv. 5–7	94	viii. 11	111
xiv. 6	95	viii 32	115
xiv 7	cf. 96	ix 5	61, 68
xiv. 8	94	I Cor i 3	cf. 110 *bis*
xiv 9	80, 94, 95 *quater*, 96, 97, cf. 96	i 23	113
		i. 24	77, 78
xiv 10, 11	80	i. 27	49
xiv 10	96, 97, cf. 96 *bis*	ii. 11	78, cf. 44
		viii. 5	cf. 31
xiv. 11	44, 96, 97 *ter*	ix. 1	68
xiv 16	47, 98, cf 29	x. 11	71
xiv 28	46, 65	xi 3	66
xv 1	98	xi. 19	cf. 50
xv 15	cf. 43	xii 4	cf 26
xvi 26	cf. 34	xiii 3	cf 26
xvi 13	116, cf 28, 59	xiii 12	64, cf. 71, 72
xvi 14	98	xv. 3, 4	cf 29, 111, 116
xvi 15	74, cf. 98	xv 3	69, 112
xvi. 28	95, 97	xv. 5–7	cf. 69
xvii. 1	cf. 98	xv. 8	69
xvii 2	34, cf 74	xv. 24, 25	34
xvii 3	cf. 31	xv 24	cf. 35
xvii. 4	cf 68	xv. 27	34
xvii 6	73	xv. 28	34, cf. 35, 74
xvii 11	cf. 98	Gal i. 1	110
xvii. 15	cf. 98	iii 13	113
xvii. 24	cf 36, 38	iii. 26	cf. 59
xix 13	cf. 73	iv. 27	cf. 49
xix 26	cf 93	Eph i 17	111
xix 28	cf 71	iv 8, 9	cf. 116
xx 17	99, 111	iv 10	cf. 60
xx 31	99 *bis*	v 8	60
xxi. 2	cf. 69	Phil. ii 6	42
Acts i 11	cf, 116	ii. 7	cf. 55

INDEX OF QUOTATIONS

	PAGE		PAGE
Col. 1. 15	cf. 40	1 John 1. 3	110
1 Thess. 1. 9	cf. 60	ii 22	110, 117
v. 5	60	iii 1	cf. 74
1 Tim. 1. 17	69	iii 23	110
ii 5	108	iv 15	117
vi. 16	66, 68 *bis*, 72, cf. 69	v 1	110
		v 8	98, cf 117
Heb ii. 7	cf. 46, 72 *ter*, 92 *bis*	v 10	cf. 117
		v 12	117
vii. 3	cf. 79	Rev 1 8	74
1 John 1. 1	67, 68, cf 66, 68 *bis*, 106	xix 6	73, 74 *bis*
		xix. 13	74

EXTERNAL SOURCES

Creeds, 28 *ter*, 29 *bis*, 105, 111
Donatus 1 1, cf. 41

Tertullian, *De praeser. haer* 27, cf 29 *bis*

INDEX OF LATIN WORDS

abundare: *ex abundanti*, 68 n. 1
adhuc · (with comparative), 57 n. 3, 58 n 3
(= *insuper, praeterea*), 93 n. 1
adnuntialis, 100 n 3
adtinet (omitted), 87 n 2
alias (= *aliter*), 26 n 2
alius alius a (*ab*), 44 n 3, 46 n 4, 76 n 1
apex, 45 n. 1

capitulum, 35 n 1
censere, 38 n. 1, 112 n 3
commentus, 28 n. 1
condicere, 73 n. 4

dicere (omitted), 47 n. 1, 107 n 1
dilectus (= agapetos), 82 n. 1
diuersus ex diuerso, 63 n 1, 67 n. 1
dum (= *cum*), 117 n. 2

esse: missing participle of, 25 n. 1
excidere, 74 n 4
exponere (= *deponere*), 99 n 1

facies, 65 n 2
fides (= *fideles*), 52 n. 2

hactenus, 104 n 2

ibidem (of time), 69 n 1
inde (= "therefore"), 91 n 1
iniectio, 104 n 3

iniuria (= "damage," "harm"), 114 n. 3
interpretari (passive), 105 n. 4
iubere (c. dat.), 57 n 2

ne (indirect interrog), 86 n. 1
nec (in prohibitive clause), 70 n. 1
non (= *ne*), 114, n. 4

obducere, 104 n 1
oratio (confused with *ratio*), 37 n 1

persona, 32 n. 2
pertinet (omitted), 87 n. 2
plane, 108 n. 1
porro (= *sed*), 75 n. 2
post (pregnant use), 98 n. 1
praedicare, 105 n 2
praescriptio, 29 n 3
prolatio, 43 n 1

qualis quale est ut, 92 n. 4
quam (= *nisi*), 113, n 2
quando (= "whereas"), 31 n. 4; (= "since"), 52 n. 3
quanti (= *quot*), 81 n. 3
quatenus (= "because"), 74 n. 1
quia (= *ut*), 60 n. 1

refrigerare (intrans), 72 n. 3
repraesentare, 53 n 1
retractatus, 30 n. 1, 54 n. 1

sacramentum, 30 n 2
sermonalis, 36 n 5
si (= *num*), 88 n. 1

INDEX OF LATIN WORDS

si forte (= *fortasse*), 64 n. 2
silua, 81 n. 1
sonare (= *praedicare, significare*), 32 n. 1, 46 n. 3
sonitus (= "meaning"), 80 n. 3
sternere (metaphorically), 71 n. 1
struere, 44 n. 1

substantia, 30 n. 4
sustinere (with participle), 59 n. 1

traducere, 27 n. 3

utpote, 54 n. 5
utrumne—an, 106 n. 2

NOTES ON THE TEXT

Pp. 34 n 1, 37 n. 1, 54 n. 5, 56 nn. 1, 3, 57 n. 4, 58 n. 1, 60 n. 1, 64 n. 2, 66 n. 1, 69 n. 2, 70 n. 3, 74 n. 4, 80 n. 3, 81 n. 2, 100 nn. 2, 5, 101 n. 2, 105 n. 2, 109 n. 2, 112 n. 5, 114 nn. 5, 6, 116 n. 1.

www.ingramcontent.com/pod-product-compliance
Lightning Source LLC
Chambersburg PA
CBHW070506100426
42743CB00010B/1779